The Art of Manifesting
A 28-day Moon Planner

by Melissa Tessaro

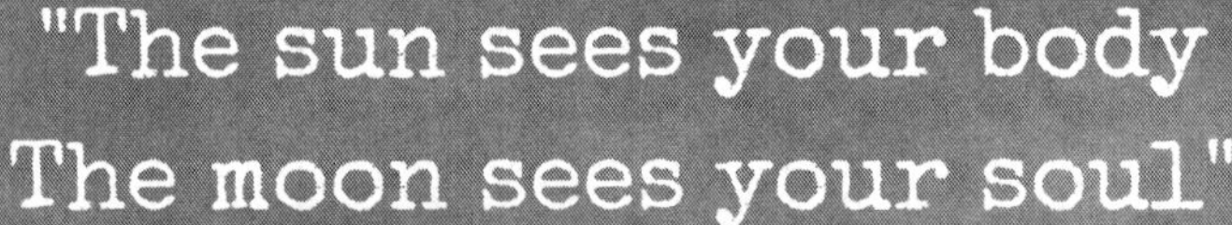

Cover design by Melissa Tessaro
Book design by Melissa Tessaro

Printed in Great Britain

"The bird who dares to fall
is the bird that learns to *fly* "
It's time to remember
who you really are.

Note from the author:

To receive the most value from this workbook you will need to know how to use a pendulum to connect with your subconscious mind.

https://thedivinationpath.thinkific.com/courses/the-pendulum-healing-course

Introduction

This section forms the foundation for the journey. Learn how to use the pendulum for dowsing and creating a safe space.

The Alchemy of Success

How does your worldview and beliefs support your ability to manifest and create alchemy?

As a planet, we are slowly waking up, becoming more energetically powerful and discovering new ways of connecting to the intelligence of the universe. Within this 28 day journal you will find tools and ideas to help you with self-empowerment, inner growth and a pathway to manifesting mastery.

The keys, codes and messages are within, as we wake up at a cellular level and learn to focus our energy we are able to gain information at lightning speed. We can also change our world view and paradigm to stretch the boundaries of what is possible beyond linear time and space.

There are many ways of manipulating energy but the fastest I know of is by using the pendulum, a tool that costs very little in comparison to the information, energy and metaphysical transformation it can give you or your clients.

This journal and journey will give you a powerful toolkit for manifesting using the pendulum to access your subconscious energy patterns, beliefs and behaviours.

Endless possibility, potential and adventure await.

The alchemist's *manifesting toolkit*

A pendulum	*A pendulum will enable you to gain clarity, receive answers from within the subconscious, change timelines, and clear blocks to manifesting.*
Curiosity	*A willingness to look at the universe and your place within it with new insight and wonder. Those that see the universe as a playground to experiment with and take risks will find the journey fun and progress faster.*
Time	*Time to focus on yourself, put yourself first, journal and find inspiration, insights and ideas. Each day will require doing an exercise and journalling which will support you energetically through this journey.*
Water	*Keep hydrated, water holds conscious awareness so you can imprint pendulum commands into water and it will hold memory, this will directly affect your cells, tissues and DNA. You can use crystals or the words with crystals for water imprinting as well.*
Safe space	*When working with higher vibrational energy such as with the pendulum it is a necessity to create a safe space to work in each time you use it. A ritual will be given for this to follow or you can use your own.*
The Moon	*The moon or any planetary energy is a key element when manifesting. When we connect and align our actions with the celestial cycles of the moon this maximises our manifesting power and provides a focus and roadmap for transformation.*
Your energy system	*Your mind, body and soul is your most powerful tool for manifesting, the body is a receiver and activator of information and light code awareness. Your voice contains sacred geometry at a higher dimensional reality. Your body and energy system is key. Keep it healthy.*

Ideas, Concepts & Words

Everything in the universe is energy and intelligent matter. Human emotions are powerful, timelines are fluid and easily changeable, time is not linear.

We are more powerful than we have been led to believe, self-belief and trust are energetic keys that will transport you fast to new ways, worlds and timelines.

Intelligent wisdom and energy are all around us to guide us. Some of the key concepts in this journal are below:

Words Words are energetic thought forms with the power and energy to create healing, change timelines and activate manifestations

Commands Structured sentences used with a pendulum for divination, healing and manifesting, they can either be clearing commands or activating commands. Clearing commands will be used with the pendulum counterclockwise and activating commands will be used clockwise. Commands can either be said in your mind or out loud.

Imprinting Activating or energetically restructuring the energy and frequency of something else with intention, using a pendulum or crystals. It is a good idea to test how stable, beneficial, and healing imprinted water is.

Programming Think of your energy and memory system like a computer which can be defragged, cleared and programmed with positive intentions. You can also shorten a long list of intentions and use one pendulum spin for many commands, this is also programming.

Vibration Everything in the universe vibrates at an atomic level, one key to manifesting is vibrating at the frequency of that which you want to manifest, this means clearing old beliefs, worries and fears at the subconscious level. This is easy and fun to do with the pendulum.

Matter All matter can be seen as holographic in nature and can be changed and transformed according to our intentions and beliefs. This is where timeline jumping comes into play. It is my belief we jump timelines each day so having a positive outlook, expectation and vibration will enable this to happen faster. You can also command this to occur.

Consciousness At some level we are energetic streams of pure consciousness that can access intelligence and wisdom of any frequency in the universe, this is also called channelling. Using the pendulum can open up new channels of wisdom and information.

WORDS MATTER & WORDS CREATE MATTER

Words are creative forces of intelligent vibration, energy & frequency. The words you use when pendulum healing really do matter.

Words are energy fields in and of themselves, they can shift worlds, open doorways, access new information energy streams & contain magic and power.

Throughout time mages, witches and alchemists use ritual with words to create energetic frequencies and manifest magic. Words hold intelligent power and create thoughtforms that can be harmful or healing.

Spin the pendulum over the words LOVE and HATE to see how the vibration of the word affects the spin of the pendulum, it is connecting to the energetic vibration contained within the word.

I once spun a word into water and thought I was enhancing the energetic frequency of the water but the word I used had double meanings, one being the vibration of a Greek monster! Needless to say after a week of rapidly going downhill I had to clear that vibration from my energy system and start again.

A list of crystal words hold as much power for healing than the original crystal, the same for flower essences and colour frequencies. This works in the same way as the idea that we can receive healing through a photograph.

This is just my belief which is why it may work so powerfully for me. Test the healing benefits of some words using the pendulum and say, "Show me the healing benefit of the vibration behind this word please".

See what happens for different words and pictures. You can do this with a 0 - 100% chart or dowsing over the word. A weakening/non-beneficial vibration will cause the pendulum to spin counter-clockwise and a positive vibration clockwise.

Using a pendulum
to fast-track manifesting

Using a pendulum will fast-track your manifesting process by using dowsing as a tool for gaining information within your subconscious level of reality. The subconscious is the realm of the non-physical, non-local and non-linear realm of existence.

This means that you can tap into your thoughts, feelings, beliefs and perceptions of yourself and the universe, test to see if they are blocking or empowering you and change any limitation from within the subconscious mind.

The subconsious
is a powerhouse of energy for transformation

- *directly connects you to divine inspiration*
- *remembers everything from this and other lives*
- *creates positive or negative patterns of behaviour*
- *uses imagery, metaphor and symbols*
- *stores our subconscious beliefs*
- *runs positive or negative emotional charges*
- *holds ancestral patterns within DNA*

To use the pendulum for clearing energy

Ask to connect to your subconscious mind, higher-self, source or any positive deity or guide you wish to access answers from. Test how connected you are on a scale of 0 - 100%.

Clearing energy using a pendulum is simply a case of making a clearing statement and spinning the pendulum counterclockwise.

To use the pendulum for enhancing/activating energy

After a clearing session wait until the pendulum has stopped spinning and then replace any voids with a positive vibrational frequency such as love, power, self-worth. Dowse to see if this has worked using a 0 - 100% scale.

You can increase your manifesting powers by clearing negative emotional charges around words/situations/events/timelines

Clearing negative emotional charges

There are beneficial exercises that you can do using the pendulum that will clear frequencies and energy not aligned with the successful vision that you want to manifest in your life. Just doing these exercises will create a timeline shift upwards and manifesting much more likely to happen faster.

Some energy carries a frequency negative or positive that will be triggered when you see pictures of something or think about a past event in your life. This negative emotional charge forms a resistance in your energy body and can block you from manifesting that which you desire.

Exercise:

1. Think of an issue from your past that makes you feel uncomfortable,
2. Dowse how uncomfortable it makes you feel on a scale of 100 ________
3. Ask does this have any negative emotional charge out of 100 __________
4. Ask to connect to the root cause of this emotional charge and clear it to zero as you spin the pendulum counterclockwise using this command:

"Connect to the root cause of this memory ___ within my energy and memory system now. I connect and transform the emotional energy charge from the root cause and all associated triggers. I now clear to zero the mental, physical, emotional, behavioural and scar issue and tissue from my energy and memory system now."

5. Keep clearing and using the pendulum counterclockwise until the pendulum stops spinning. Then test using the pendulum to see if you still have a negative charge.

"Do I have a negative emotional charge around_______ memory affecting my ability to manifest?"

YES NO

Creating a safe space

It is absolutely necessary to work in a safe space when doing any form of pendulum dowsing or healing. We are connecting into higher vibrational energies and need to clear and protect the space we are working in and from.

Safety is the key foundation for all energetic and alchemical work.

When we are safe we are free to fly and create magic.

"Is there any non-beneficial energy affecting my dowsing or pendulum healing work right now?"

Use the YES and NO part of this chart to answer the question above.

If you receive a YES then ask what percentage is there of any non-beneficial energy affecting your pendulum dowsing session. The words you use are always important so be specific and say affecting any part of my dowsing or healing contained in this session.

"Clear or transmute all non-beneficial energy around myself, my pendulum, my pendulum commands and the focus of the pendulum session in this reality and all realities, timelines and dimensions now. Connect only to my own higher power, insight and wisdom now. This is instant and permanent now, every other energy is now transmuted and sent to the sun for clearing with love."

Check your percentages again after the clearing statement and if not 100% clear of all non-beneficial energy you state...

"Clear everything hidden in the shadows or in my blindspot, all energy lower than me is visible and sent to the sun now for my highest good and the highest good of all concerned."

Charts, Commands & Ideas

This section contains charts, commands and ideas for manifesting mastery and connecting with your higher self in magical ways.

Gratitude

changes how we look at the world

What % are you in alignment with the energetic frequency of gratitude today?

Use the pendulum with a 0 - 100% chart to test how aligned with these statements you are.
You can raise your vibration by simply commanding it,

"Raise vibration and appreciation of life and enable me to align with the frequency of gratitude, g race and wisdom".

Raises my vibration and makes me happier
Releases me from struggle
Opens the door to abundance
Brings new experiences to my timeline
Brings hope, joy and peace
Enables me to get things done faster
Creates optimism, growth and support

Increases my energy levels
Enables me to bounce back from setbacks
Improves my decision making
Brings me more friendships
Increases my productivity levels
Frees me from fear
Reduces insecurity and doubts

I am grateful for:

The Art of Self-Care

Your energy & time are your most important assets, how well do you value them? Use a 0 - 100% chart to test how you value yourself and your energy.

Value your energy & time?
Set energetic boundaries?
Say 'no' to things?
Find time for yourself?
Find time to have fun?
Take time out in nature?
Rest & take breaks?
Get proper sleep?
Know your limits?
Practice self-love?
Relax, meditate & reflect?
Enjoy life's journey?
Take time to create?
Do what you love?
Change what does not suit you?
Learn new ways?
Eat nourishing foods?
Clear clutter?
Banish non-beneficial energy?
Protect space energetically?

Being happy on earth

Sometimes as starseeds, empaths, and lightworkers we subconsciously don't want to be here on earth especially if we had difficult childhoods and are sensitive to other people's vibrations.

It will be harder to manifest the things you do want if you subconsciously do not want to be on earth. Get those roots down into Mother Earth and connect to her healing powers and wisdom.

Questions

What % am I able to journey here safely on Earth?	0 10 20 30 40 50 60 70 80 90 100
What % do I feel valued by others?	0 10 20 30 40 50 60 70 80 90 100
What % am I able to achieve my Soul's plans?	0 10 20 30 40 50 60 70 80 90 100
What % have I met my Soul family?	0 10 20 30 40 50 60 70 80 90 100
What % am I connected to Mother Earth?	0 10 20 30 40 50 60 70 80 90 100
What % have I found the right mentors?	0 10 20 30 40 50 60 70 80 90 100
What % do I need to protect myself from other's energy?	0 10 20 30 40 50 60 70 80 90 100
What % do I feel safe in my body?	0 10 20 30 40 50 60 70 80 90 100
What % do I subconsciously want to be on Earth?	0 10 20 30 40 50 60 70 80 90 100

Commands

Clear to zero subconscious neglect, pain, and suffering & illuminate my life path clearly
Enable me to participate in life's experiences with joy
Radiate blessings into my timeline and lifetime
Release deep Soul burdens both real and imagined
Clear energy stream of self-punishment & self-hatred
Find peace and deep restructuring with happiness
Clear all patterns and programs not serving me now
Enable me to fully co-operate with Mother Earth
Clear to zero doubts, fears and misery keeping me trapped, small and limited.
I shed that past now, I walk forwards with light

A power & presence blessing

"Connect to, access & restore
peace, patience, presence & power
within my NOW timeline and
lifetime for my highest health,
wealth and energetic path.
Bless all my steps today
as I find inner strength &
energetic wisdom."

Clearing the energetic frequency of blame, shame & fear

I send thanks to Mother Earth for birthing us and providing support
I now end all running fear programs, I leave behind the shadow of the past
I am no longer ashamed of who I am and what I stand for
All layers of doubt, shame, fear, and low confidence are dissolved in this lifetime
and timeline now. I step through a new doorway and activate a powerful new future now

I thank my three teachers, blame, shame & fear for their wisdom and let them go
I now release all past pain, persecution, fear, doubt, and trauma from cellular memories
My cells are free and alive, my DNA activates with self-love and wisdom and
receives guidance from my higher self, my new journey is filled with fun, joy, friendship
and freedom.

My solar plexus energy is activated and new boundaries are set with strength
I access the physical activation of source within my energy and memory system
I allow myself to know who I am and where I am going
My cells dance with joy, freedom, and wisdom
I am fully awake and aware and step out of the shadows
My higher self, soul group and monad join me on this new path

I radiate inner peace
I radiate inner power
I radiate inner strength
my journey has begun ...

Moon Charged Water
energy dowsing chart

The moon's energy has been associated with magic, healing, fertility, beauty & abundance.

Making and using moon water is a powerful alchemical process that holds much power, insight and illumination. Lunar water activation using intention or with the pendulum will hold huge potential for self-mastery as it will bring hidden awareness to the surface for clearing, shifting, repairing or healing.

Use this dowsing chart to assess which moon phase is most powerful for each of these topics you might want to make lunar water for. Use the dowsing phrase below or make up your own.

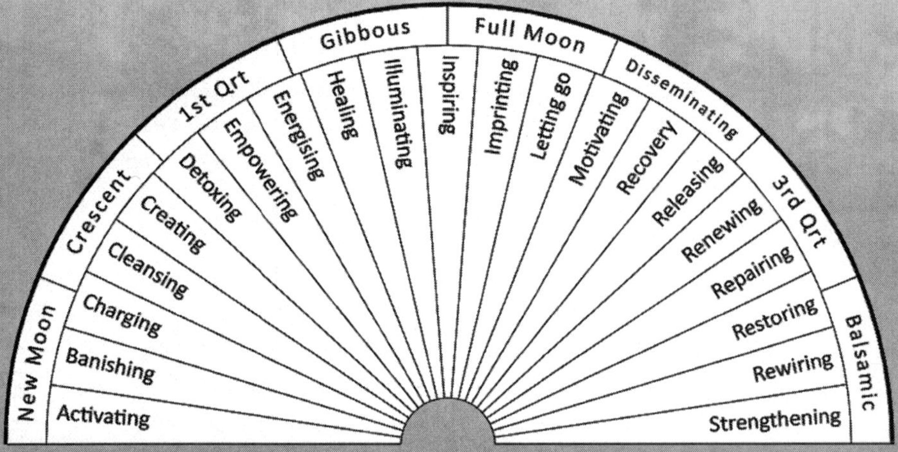

Magic will come into my life this ________ moon by making the energetic vibration & frequency of ________ water

When the moon is full in different signs of the zodiac you can also use this knowledge to energise and empower your water or you can metaphysically add the energy of one of the planets to your water with the intention or calling in the energy using the pendulum and a clockwise spin.

Aries - Courage with positivity for practical purposes
Taurus - Stability & power
Gemini - Evolution & revolution
Cancer - Self-love & healing
Leo - Personal power, creativity & luck
Virgo - Planning & action
Libra - Balance & harmony
Scorpio - Banishing & disconnecting
Sagittarius - Transforming from within
Capricorn - Career evolving & business
Aquarius - Innovation & expansion
Pisces - Psychic awareness & hidden inner work

Commands for Procrastination

I release all procrastination patterns & the energy of being stuck
I clear all subconscious non-beneficial energy keeping me powerless
I remove all worries, fear, and anxiety around making the wrong choice
I collapse fears of being too responsible or doing the wrong thing
I release all my past life negative energetic karmic & generational energy
Enable me to realise the time is now to take action on my goals
All fear, blame and shame lifts from my energy system now
Allow me to realise I have everything I need to move forwards
I call in the wisdom of my higher self to activate new action
I send love to my inner child and say it's safe to act now
I release the root cause keeping me stuck in this life
Enable me to know how to prioritise my time and energy
I am easily focused on my goals and know I can succeed
I release all guilt at not having followed my dreams sooner
My cells, tissues and organs release inertia, inaction, doubt, and worry
I easily take small steps each day towards my goals
I gently release all subconscious self-sabotage now
I call on self-confidence, patience, wisdom and
mastery to walk with me on my journey now
I know that I am magical

How to access divine magic

Clear limiting beliefs	0 10 20 30 40 50 60 70 80 90 100
Open heart center	0 10 20 30 40 50 60 70 80 90 100
Activate chakras	0 10 20 30 40 50 60 70 80 90 100
Clear auric field	0 10 20 30 40 50 60 70 80 90 100
Write affirmations	0 10 20 30 40 50 60 70 80 90 100
Create a new timeline	0 10 20 30 40 50 60 70 80 90 100
Ask guides to help	0 10 20 30 40 50 60 70 80 90 100
Use crystals	0 10 20 30 40 50 60 70 80 90 100
Use runes	0 10 20 30 40 50 60 70 80 90 100
Use water imprinting	0 10 20 30 40 50 60 70 80 90 100
Let go of the old	0 10 20 30 40 50 60 70 80 90 100
Detox	0 10 20 30 40 50 60 70 80 90 100
Balance	0 10 20 30 40 50 60 70 80 90 100
Stand in own power	0 10 20 30 40 50 60 70 80 90 100
Visualisations	0 10 20 30 40 50 60 70 80 90 100
Clear past conditioning	0 10 20 30 40 50 60 70 80 90 100
Write affirmations in future	0 10 20 30 40 50 60 70 80 90 100
Vision board	0 10 20 30 40 50 60 70 80 90 100
Subconscious commands	0 10 20 30 40 50 60 70 80 90 100
Spend more money	0 10 20 30 40 50 60 70 80 90 100
Be more grateful	0 10 20 30 40 50 60 70 80 90 100
Be more positive	0 10 20 30 40 50 60 70 80 90 100
Be more focused	0 10 20 30 40 50 60 70 80 90 100
Be more relaxed	0 10 20 30 40 50 60 70 80 90 100
Purify water	0 10 20 30 40 50 60 70 80 90 100
Follow intention	0 10 20 30 40 50 60 70 80 90 100
Watch for the signs	0 10 20 30 40 50 60 70 80 90 100

This exact command netted the author £1,800 the day after she spun this into her cellular energy and memory consciousness in this timeline and lifetime for the highest wealth activation.

"I activate and walk through a living doorway of abundance now. This doorway is a stream of alchemical sacred geometric patterns & light language affecting my ability to receive abundance on every level. Great shifts are happening now in my energy system. I am upgrading and attuned to abundance. I leave behind all drama, poverty, and misuse of power in relation to money matters. I reclaim my wealth self now."

The metaphysics & psychology *of* Aligning with luck

Professor Richard Wiseman found that lucky people believed the universe was more abundant, were open to possibilities and expected good fortune to come their way than non-lucky people.

- What % do you believe the universe is abundant? 0 10 20 30 40 50 60 70 80 90 100
- What % are you open to possibilities? 0 10 20 30 40 50 60 70 80 90 100
- Expect good fortune to come your way? 0 10 20 30 40 50 60 70 80 90 100
- Open-minded 0 10 20 30 40 50 60 70 80 90 100
- Willing to try new things? 0 10 20 30 40 50 60 70 80 90 100

LUCKY PEOPLE	UNLUCKY PEOPLE
Found it easy to socialise	Were neurotic
Extraverted	Anxious/Worried
Connected with others	Had tunnel vision
Had high expectations	Not open
Left comfort zone	Fixated on one thing
Maintained relationships	Introverted
Were generally optimistic	Expected bad luck

Do you think about luck?
Can we creatively call in aspects of luck using charms, colours, symbols?
Do you need to disconnect from any unlucky vibrations NOW?

Can we switch on or off the energy of luck?
Can we transmute the energy of unlucky to lucky?
Can you dowse to see if there is any bad luck in your timeline? Birthchart? Past lives?

A pendulum command to transform the energy of luck:

"Connect to and transmute any unlucky thought forms, energy, curses, vows and hexes within my energy field and timeline now. Clear anything negatively affecting my ability to create, receive and manifest LUCK and wealth in my now timeline. Remove all forms and signatures of BAD LUCK and replace with GOOD LUCK in my now timeline for highest wealth."

Becoming visible

Releasing commands for visibility

I forgive myself, I forgive myself, I forgive myself
Release all inner tension, fear, and doubts keeping me small
Release all fears of criticism from myself or others holding me back
Remove all worries and expectations around being judged
I release all power struggles from myself and others blocking my progress
Remove all doubts around my ability picked up from others
Remove all negative ego transmissions from mind, body, and soul
Release all echoes of past dramas, attachments, and loss affecting me now
Remove all blocks around having success and losing it

Use the pendulum counterclockwise and repeat these commands

Restoring commands for visibility

Allow me to find it easy to project my personal power and wisdom freely
I am free to show my inner child that I am responsible for my destiny
Transform me into someone who easily tries new things
Allow me to make mistakes and know that life is a journey of discovery
I easily step forth, accept my power and activate it now
I see clearly and action upon my vision
Enable me to have fun and light with the challenges of life
Increase my courage, love and self-belief to the highest possible levels
Enable me to have clarity and perspective to see the bigger picture
I receive help from human and non-human divine elements and elementals

Use the pendulum clockwise and repeat these commands

Goal Setting *tips*

"Goal setting is the process of deciding what you want to accomplish and then devising a plan to achieve the desired result."

1. Choose worthwhile goals	0 10 20 30 40 50 60 70 80 90 100
2. Choose achievable goals	0 10 20 30 40 50 60 70 80 90 100
3. Make them specific	0 10 20 30 40 50 60 70 80 90 100
4. Commit to them	0 10 20 30 40 50 60 70 80 90 100
5. Make them public	0 10 20 30 40 50 60 70 80 90 100
6. Prioritize them	0 10 20 30 40 50 60 70 80 90 100
7. Stay motivated	0 10 20 30 40 50 60 70 80 90 100
8. Set deadlines	0 10 20 30 40 50 60 70 80 90 100
9. Evaluate them	0 10 20 30 40 50 60 70 80 90 100
10. Reward success	0 10 20 30 40 50 60 70 80 90 100
11. Clear self-sabotage	0 10 20 30 40 50 60 70 80 90 100
12. Ask for clarity from guides	0 10 20 30 40 50 60 70 80 90 100
13. Ask for clarity from higher self	0 10 20 30 40 50 60 70 80 90 100
14. Ask for clarity from subconscious	0 10 20 30 40 50 60 70 80 90 100
15. Spin the outcome into your timeline	0 10 20 30 40 50 60 70 80 90 100
16. Write affirmations around the goals	0 10 20 30 40 50 60 70 80 90 100
17. What % is your subconscious in alignment with your goal	0 10 20 30 40 50 60 70 80 90 100

"Enable me to experience
grounded magic with
cosmic wisdom in everyday life.
I easily connect with the
abundance of life."

Candle Magic

ritual for working with money energy

Rituals set focus, awareness and harness energy. You can use colour with candle magic, water imprinting or connecting to the consciousness and energy of the colour using a pendulum to empower your moon rituals. You can also imagine the candle in your mind if you don't have one.

White *cleanses the energetic frequency of money*
Red *boosts the energy power of money on your timeline*
Pink *increases love of money & energy attraction*
Yellow *find creative ways of bringing money in*
Blue *receive new wisdom around receiving money*
Green *increases luck in your timeline*
Black *will banish bad luck in your timeline*
Orange *increases positive association with money*
Purple *enhances inner power, potential & flow*
Brown *connects with the abundance of mother earth*
Grey *increases clarification of life path*
Gold *raises success around work/life path/goals*
Turquoise *radiates calm around the energy of money*
Silver *expands energy consciousness around money*

Use the dowsing chart below to see which colour energy frequency you most need relating to wealth or manifesting right now.

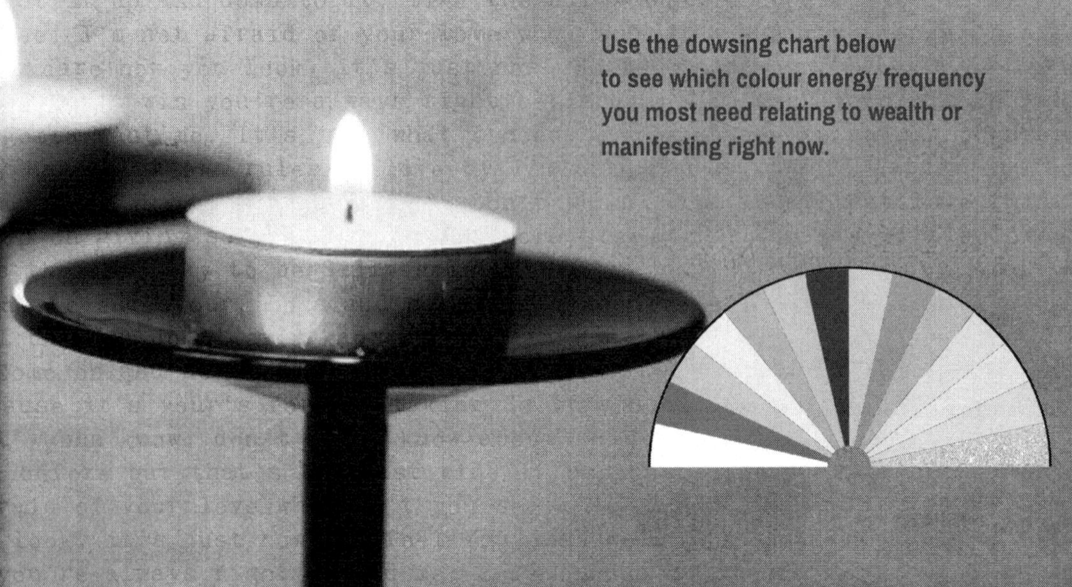

Your higher self

Your higher self has all the answers and knows your life path. It is your choice whether to connect with your higher self/soul when dowsing and using the pendulum but I strongly advise it.

When we identify with our problems, doubts and fears we lose sight of the fact that we are multi-dimensional beings with intelligence, awareness and insight that goes far beyond our 3rd-dimensional reality on earth. It is highly possible and beneficial to connect to your higher self using the pendulum for answers and illumination that you just cannot access with conscious thought alone.

To connect with your higher self you simply have to ask to do so. Check using a 0 - 100% chart that you are only connected with your higher self/source or a higher vibrational aspect of you that is aware of more than 3D reality.

It is thought that as we raise our vibrational frequency both individually and as a collective our ego will eventually merge with the higher self and we will be free of lower 3D worries and concerns.

Questions:

Will merging with my higher self allow me to create the life I want?

What % can I ask my higher self for more inspiration and support?

What % am I guided by LOVE over FEAR?

What % am I hearing messages from my higher self?

Write a letter *to your future timeline*

Ask to speak to the energy of the next 6 months. You can ask for anything to happen or just clear blocks, doubts, fears and struggles to make room for a new beginning. You can test using the pendulum to see if your timeline has changed for the better after this exercise.

example:

"I am now speaking to the energy of my timeline for the next 6 months. I am asking pain, shame and struggle to leave my energy and memory system now. I recallibrate my timeline for success. I choose to focus on higher vibrations and happier times. I am attracted to all that makes me happy, fullfilled and joyful. I am creative and masterful. I clear all inherited timelines of trauma, drama, misery, rage distrust, bitterness and envy and replace with love. I heal and integrate unloved aspects of my soul and with it I reclaim abundance inheritance now."

Clarity & Focus

Pendulum commands

I release all self-doubt, fear, and confusion picked up in any lifetime now
Enable me to release complaining around being uncertain
Release my energy from others who doubt my abilities
Release all non-beneficial energy clouding my thoughts
Huge problems in my mind are replaced with clarity
The fog of despair is removed from my brain pathway
I gently release all lack of focus and overwhelm now
Release all family and generational pressures affecting my way of life
Enable me to release all beliefs and insecurities holding me back
I release all vague ideas and activate clarity from my higher self
Easily release the pain and trauma from past judgements

I am a powerful being who is able to create the life of my dreams
Enable me to step up and be responsible for my own life
I experience clarity of thought and crystal clear illumination
My energy and flow are in perfect alignment
My clarity, focus and drive make me a leader in my field
I am calm and focused on my future
I am brilliant

Grounding & Balance

You receive more wisdom when you are grounded & balanced

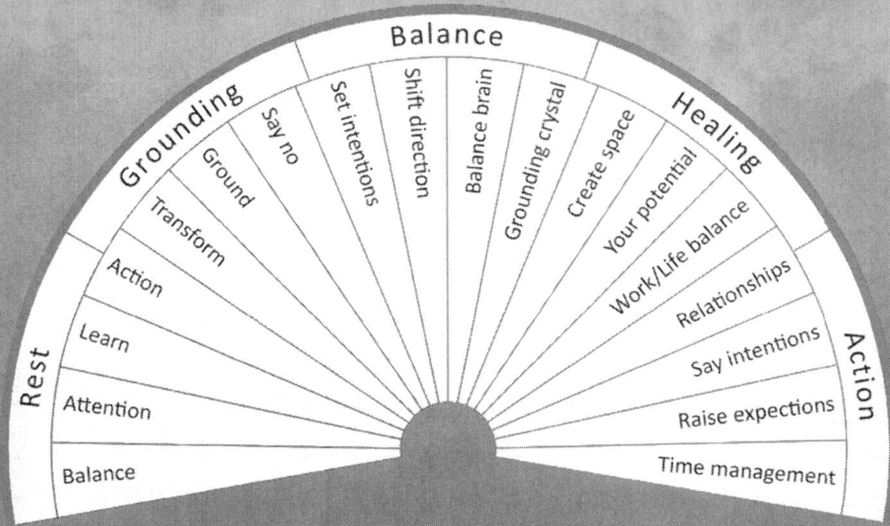

Notes:

"Where there is no balance there is also no joy." R Daffeh

The Lunar Cycle Chart

full moon

gibbous moon

disseminating moon

first quarter

third quarter

waxing moon

waning moon

crescent moon

balsamic moon

new moon

Using the lunar cycle as a dowsing chart

Dowse with the pendulum ask, "Which cycle is it best for me to __________"

See where the pendulum swings to and make note.

New Moon - planting seeds, new beginnings, rituals, creating a vision, setting intentions
Crescent Moon - energy with focus, planning, ground energy into action, goal setting
First Quarter - gather resources, take action, draw power from elements, release fears
Gibbous Moon - refine, assess, energetically powerful, patience, protection
Full Moon - manifesting, dreaming big, guidance, illumination, self-care, higher powers
Disseminating Moon - release the past, ancestral healing, cellular repair, addictions
Third Quarter - letting go, releasing, gratitude, clear NBE, limiting beliefs, cutting cords
Balsamic Moon - rest, restore, retreat, rejuvenate, give thanks, blessings

Waning Moon - Energetically clearing with healing
Waxing Moon - Increasing wellness & vitality

The Lunar Cycle
dowsing questions

Use this questionnaire with the lunar cycle chart to dowse which time is it most energetically powerful to take action on these areas of life. You can also check the percentage it would benefit you to take action.

The Self

New beginnings ____________
Self-care ____________
Creativity ____________
Making decisions ____________
Standing in power ____________
Subconscious ____________

Divination & Guidance

Divination ____________
Manifesting rituals ____________
Using sigils ____________
Planetary healing ____________
Higher self energy ____________

Going deeper

Mind control ____________
Womb healing ____________
Genetic healing ____________
Toxic relationships ____________
Inner child healing ____________
Deep fears ____________
Archetypes ____________
Timeline healing ____________
Burnout ____________

Healing

Cellular healing ____________
Starting diet ____________
Clearing toxins ____________
Organ healing ____________
Chakra healing ____________
Meridian healing ____________

Career

Looking for a job ____________
Collaborating ____________
Career plans ____________
Making decisions ____________
Organising ____________
Tracking progress ____________
Marketing ____________
Overcoming obstacles ____________

The past

Clearing the past ____________
Ancestral clearing ____________
Genetic lineage ____________
Womb healing ____________
Bad habits ____________

The Rose Compass
wisdom chart

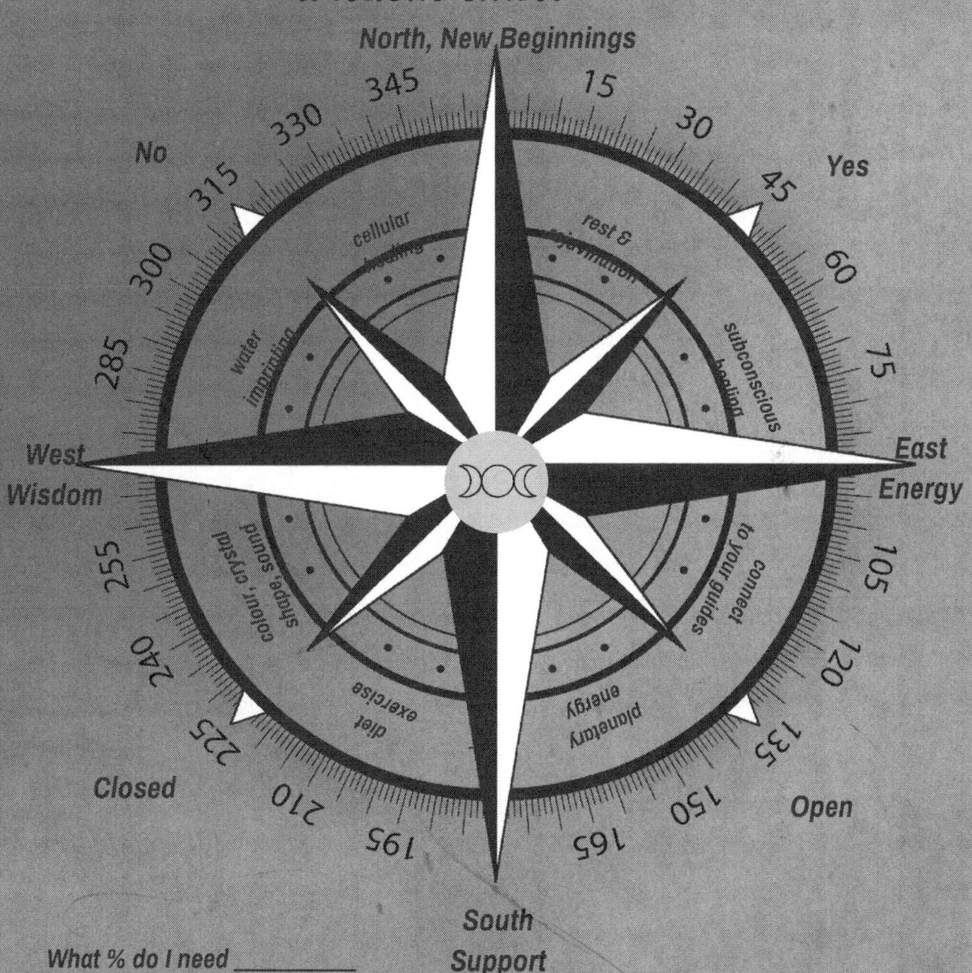

What % do I need _________
for my highest health, and well-being?

Cellular healing	*low medium high*
Rest & rejuvination	*low medium high*
Subconscious healing	*low medium high*
Connect with guides	*low medium high*
Planetary energy	*low medium high*
Diet/Exercise	*low medium high*
Colour/crystal/shape	*low medium high*
Water imprinting	*low medium high*

Use the dowsing chart to ask which energy would be most beneficial for you right now. You can use the numbers as a percentage system to measure the energy.

MAKING LUNAR WATER

Dr Emoto & Dr J Benvenista have both discovered that water is capable of carrying imprinted frequencies as patterns of energy and information.

This is called water imprinting or structured water and people sell this for large amounts of money. You can make your own lunar imprinted water with the energy and frequency of your desires or positive intent.

The water will hold the energetic frequency of the astrological day it was imprinted with, the intention and energy of the person making the water and the elements of mother nature.

Imprint positive intention and instructions into your water with a pendulum, crystals or just your heart-based energy.

Water can help with your inner journey, blessing water really does change its energetic structure and frequency. You can drink imprinted water for cellular health and vitality.

Why not imprint positive instructions into your DNA or use crystals around the outside of the jar to power up the water.

Charging water with the energy of the moon is an alchemical tool for magical awareness and transformation.

Cosmic Light Commands

Recreate rainbow light frequency on earth
Activate the golden frequency of light ascension & knowledge
Manifest the highest & best timeline through the galaxy for all
Enable us to use our gifts & awareness to bring laughter, joy and wonder daily
Clear our focus, doubts and re-direct our energy through the core crystal grids

Accelerate the SUN, MOON and EARTH cosmic dance of pure wonder & light
As we step into our divinely assisted flow we activate, raise, and expand our energy awareness of love, peace, and harmony.

Accelerate conscious expansion globally & awareness of the power of TIME
Increase our ability to hold light code forms, information & messages
Increase our ability & awareness to perceive our own light
Enable us to find others like us who perceive & activate magic $ light with innovation, open vision & delight.

We are all blessed
We activate cosmic rays of light

Some days you just have to create your own *sunshine*

I am a powerful soul manifestor and creator of wealth magic
Clear to zero any soul struggles relating to creating wealth now
Clear any hinderances, hidden blocks, traps, fears, and doubts from self or others
Connect to any hereditary, ancestral, genetic, galactic restrictions & clear
Raise my belief in my innate mastery and ability to consciously create wealth

It is now super easy for me to attract wealth into my now lifetime and timeline
I shed old baggage and struggles around money, finances, and ability to create wealth
A new dawn and a re-birth of abundance has now begun for me
Clear to zero old beliefs of lack, scarcity, and lack residing in control programs & imprints
Frustration, disappointment, fear, and confusion tied to money is dissolved now
I see opportunity and I am free to create and make wealth for myself and my family

I clear and de-program all poverty and slavery consciousness keeping me stuck
I am now open to receiving more than before, increase prosperity flow in all areas of life
Clear negative unhelpful money karma from my energy and memory system now
Rejuvenate my innate ability to build the life I desire, I am manifesting with freedom now

Ask to receive a message from the consciousness of wealth:

"I am directly connected to your self-worth, how you value your life. Call on me to clear blocks, I am right here."

The art of tracking time

Use this chart to check when something is likely to happen or manifest in your timeline and for tracking goals and tasks.

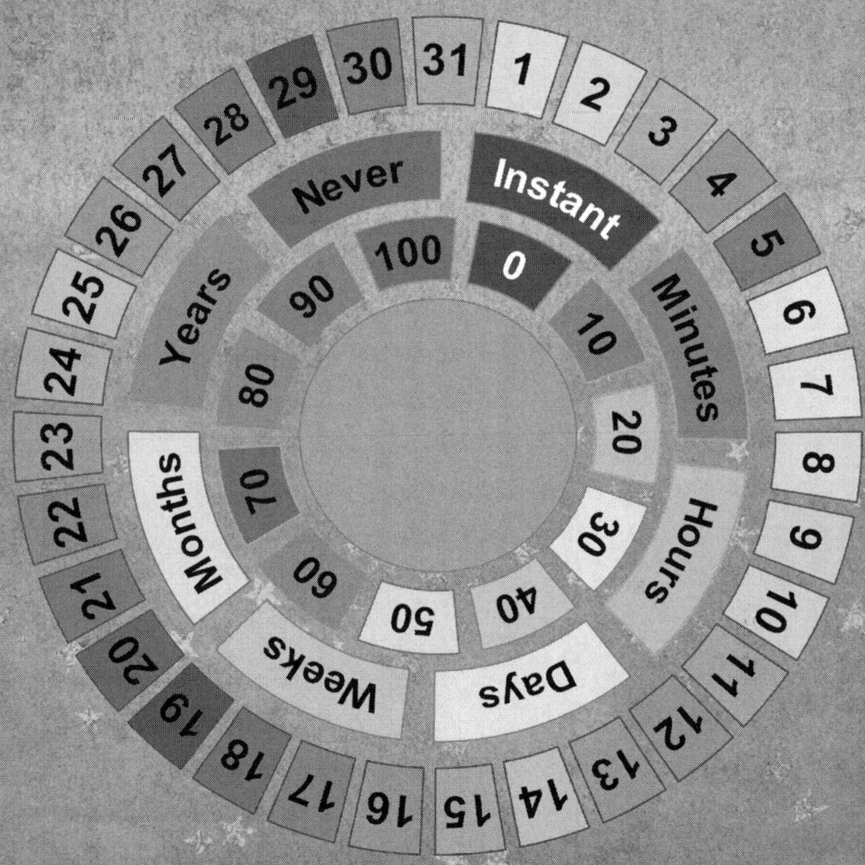

Ideas for using this chart to track, test and check how long to do something around these ideas

Task tracking	0 10 20 30 40 50 60 70 80 90 100	Good habits	0 10 20 30 40 50 60 70 80 90 100
Time to manifest	0 10 20 30 40 50 60 70 80 90 100	Clearing bad habits	0 10 20 30 40 50 60 70 80 90 100
Healing	0 10 20 30 40 50 60 70 80 90 100	Internal action	0 10 20 30 40 50 60 70 80 90 100
Detoxing	0 10 20 30 40 50 90 70 80 90 100	External action	0 10 20 30 40 50 90 70 80 90 100
Goal setting	0 10 20 30 40 50 60 70 80 90 100	Setting tasks	0 10 20 30 40 50 60 70 80 90 100
Timeline information	0 10 20 30 40 50 60 70 80 90 100	Energy clearing	0 10 20 30 40 50 60 70 80 90 100
Dieting	0 10 20 30 40 50 60 70 80 90 100	Motivation	0 10 20 30 40 50 60 70 80 90 100
Rituals	0 10 20 30 40 50 90 70 80 90 100	Water imprinting	0 10 20 30 40 50 90 70 80 90 100

Magical correspondences
daily chart

You can use the energy, power and frequency of correspondences to boost your pendulum commands, strengthen manifestations or increase the energy around something you are trying to achieve.

Ask to connect to the energetic frequency of a day, a planet or a metal for fast resolution and action. Test using the pendulum that you are connected and listen for advice or just ask to connect to the energetic power and magic.

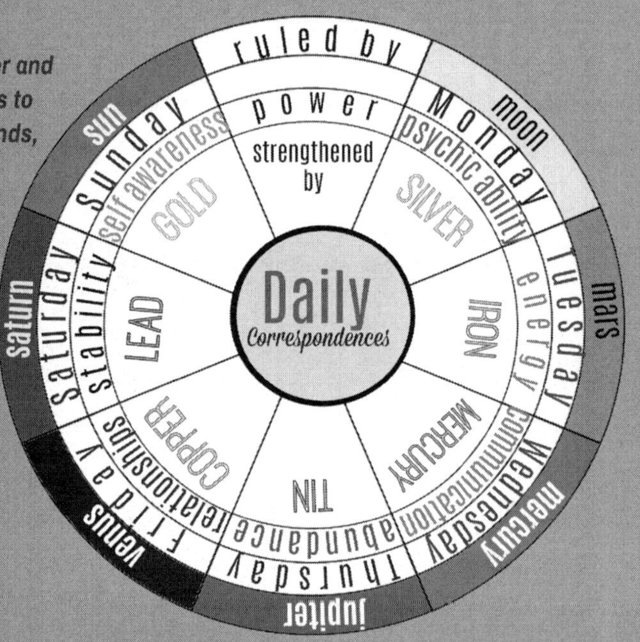

Mon	Scrying/Sigils, Dreams, Powering amulets, Water imprinting, Psychic ability, Silver - Healing & magic
Tue	Ambition, Protection, Reversing commands, Psychic attack, Strengthening affirmations Iron - Shamanic journeying & protection
Wed	Communication, Creativity, Debt, Divination, Education, Fear, Flexibility, Fortune, Luck Mercury - Mental clarity, communication & progress
Thu	Energetic Increase, Expansion, Generosity, Growth, Happiness, Healing Tin - Abundance, healing energy, rejuvenation, and regeneration
Fri	Arts, Beauty, Birth, Fertility, Friendship, Growth, Harmony, Love, Marriage, Music, Nature Copper - Energy conduction, expansion & healing
Sat	Banishment, Binding, Boundaries, Caution, Cleansing, Endings, Hidden Matters, Limitations Lead - Stability, grounding, breaking bad habit, connecting to the unconscious
Sun	Personal Achievements, Power, Promotions, Self-Expression, Spiritual Connection, Success Gold - Growth, Financial success and power

Manifesting Mastery

A journey with the moon

Welcome to the manifesting with the moon 28-day transformational planner. Each topic for the 28 days is below and corresponds to the celestial phase and journey of the moon.

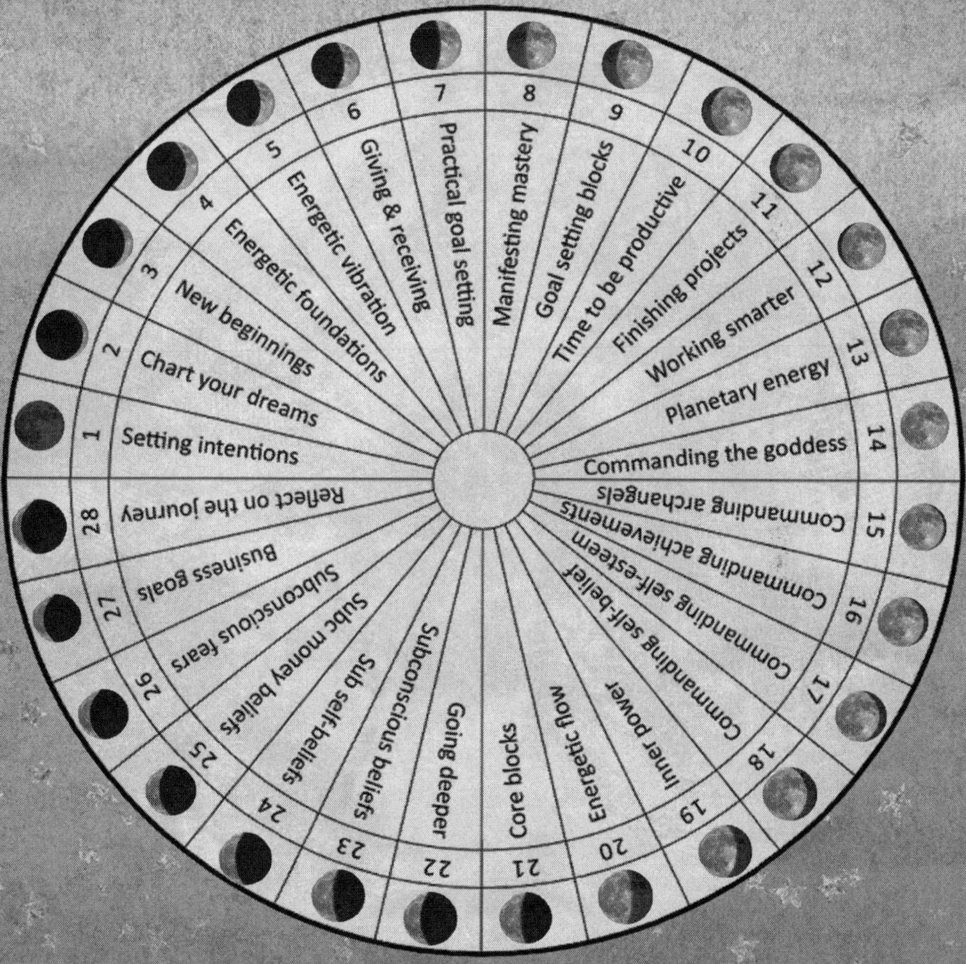

As always only accept that which resonates for you. Test pendulum commands for effectiveness Write down all your ideas and insights on your journey.Anything you do you can undo and enjoy the journey.

The Journey Begins

The 28-day journey begins connecting your vision, energy, power & focus with that of the celestial magic of the moon. Each day will guide you through an exercise and space for journalling your inner magic.

Day 1 - Setting Intentions
Day 2 - Chart your Dreams
Day 3 - New Beginnings
Day 4 - Energetic Foundations
Day 5 - Energetic Vibration
Day 6 - Giving & Receiving
Day 7 - Practical Goal Setting
Day 8 - Manifesting Mastery
Day 9 - Goal Setting Blocks
Day 10 - Time to Be Productive
Day 11 - Finishing Projects
Day 12 - Working Smarter
Day 13 - Planetary Energy
Day 14 - Commanding the Goddess
Day 15 - Commanding Archangels
Day 16 - Commanding Achievements
Day 17 - Commanding Self-esteem
Day 18 - Commanding Self-belief
Day 19 - Inner Power
Day 20 - Energetic Flow
Day 21 - Core Blocks
Day 22 - Going Deeper
Day 23 - Subconscious Beliefs
Day 24 - Subconscious Self-beliefs
Day 25 - Subconscious Money Beliefs
Day 26 - Subconscious Fears
Day 27 - Business Goals
Day 28 - Reflect on the Journey

New Moon Intentions

setting your intention

Writing a clear intention statement for the next 30 days sends a strong powerful message to the universe that you are ready, focused and able to receive success, this process will focus your conscious awareness, increase self-belief and bring your creative power into the now.

My new moon intentions are:

Ask for manifesting support & feedback from the universe. Planetary magick of Jupiter can help expansion with blessings. Use a planetary app to locate the planetary hours each day and use them for adding energy & power to your days.

Notes:

https://www.facebook.com/groups/theartofmanifesting/

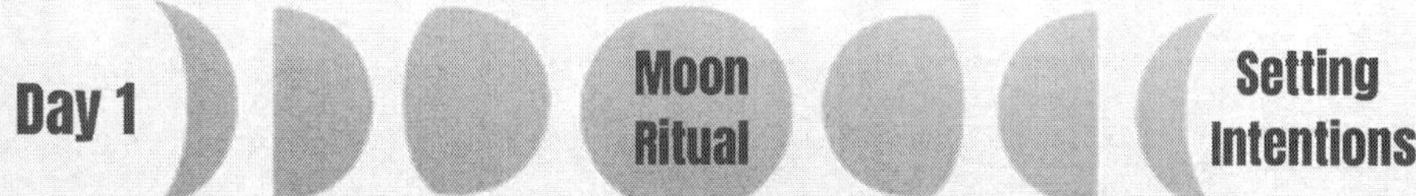

What to expect on this journey?

Day 1 is easy and is just setting your intention for this 28-day moon cycle.

It's time to believe in the power and magic of new beginnings. Everyone has the ability to manifest easily and when you increase your self-awareness & give yourself permission to shine you will find it easy to achieve miracles.

These moon ritual pages will have exercises, charts or commands to use which will focus your energy as you manifest your intentions and dreams. When we allow ourselves to be free from core issues and limitations at the subconscious level, we gain more energy, wisdom, and guidance and open up to allowing the universe to support and guide us.

Writing affirmations creates the energetic link between the inner universe and our outer reality, our link focuses our desires with action and intention. It is important that for the first five days you write your affirmations as though you have already achieved them and with a strong positive emotion and do not miss a day.

You will be clearing resistance, fears, and old beliefs on this journey which might activate suppressed emotions that come to the surface, this is natural and healing so give yourself space to energetically feel and free what comes up for you each day.

Asking questions of your subconscious mind gives valuable insight and intuition into the areas that you might need to focus on during this journey.

Questions to think/dowse around:

What % do you project negative energy into your timeline?
What % are you giving away your power?
What % are you honouring your soul gifts?
What % are you ok with being visible?
What % are you fearful of rejection?
What % is help available to you that you have not tapped into?
What % are you waiting for permission to begin the life you want to live?
What % are you waiting to be recognised by others?
What % do you recognise your zone of genius?
What % is the law of attraction working for you positively?
What % of the time do you manifest
positively ________
negatively ________

0 10 20 30 40 50 60 70 80 90 100

Day 1

Moon Planner

Setting intentions . planting seeds . new beginnings

Daily Intention:

My goals & plans:

Check your goals are:
Relevant
Achieveable
Measurable
In alignment

Tasks:

What % do I need to:

Set intentions	0 10 20 30 40 50 60 70 80 90 100
Make plans	0 10 20 30 40 50 60 70 80 90 100
Set goals	0 10 20 30 40 50 60 70 80 90 100
Set tasks	0 10 20 30 40 50 60 70 80 90 100
Best timeline	0 10 20 30 40 50 60 70 80 90 100
Write affirmations	0 10 20 30 40 50 60 70 80 90 100
Positive mindset	0 10 20 30 40 50 60 70 80 90 100

I am grateful for:

Day 2

Moon Ritual

Chart your dreams

Using a dowsing chart to clarify your dreams

My intention is:

What does your higher self want you to know? Can you receive more clarity around your intention using this chart? Yes/No

This chart will give a bit more insight regarding the intention you are setting during this moon cycle. If you dowse and ask to show you how beneficial your intention is for this particular moon cycle and note the answer.

1 2 3 4 5 6 7 8 9 10 11

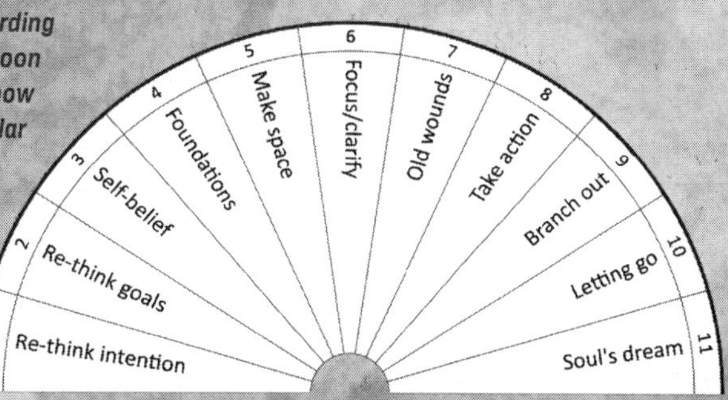

You can then decide to re-think your intention or keep it as it is.

Then ask, "Is there anything I need to know during this moon cycle relating to my intention?" NO YES

Key

1. *Dream/intention not your highest Soul's path, time to re-think for this moon cycle*
2. *Set or re-think goals that relate to your intention*
3. *Increase self-belief & ability in your power to manifest*
4. *Strengthen foundations with self-love, your inner child can help you*
5. *Make space for dreams to come in, clear clutter, discard the old*
6. *Focus and clarify your ideas, build processes, plan and streamline*
7. *Clear old wounds, others projections, fears and blocks trapping abundance*
8. *Time to take action in the real world*
9. *Branch out and collaborate with others, move out of your comfort zone*
10. *Work is done, time to let go and be patient*
11. *This is your soul's dream and mission, easily achievable for you to create magic*

Day 2

Moon Planner

Setting intentions . planting seeds . new beginnings

Daily Intention:

Most excited to plan, action & achieve:

I am reluctant to:

What % am i ?

Excited	0 10 20 30 40 50 60 70 80 90 100
Joyful	0 10 20 30 40 50 60 70 80 90 100
Nervous	0 10 20 30 40 50 60 70 80 90 100
Eager	0 10 20 30 40 50 60 70 80 90 100
Free to achieve	0 10 20 30 40 50 60 70 80 90 100
Restricted	0 10 20 30 40 50 60 70 80 90 100
Allowing	0 10 20 30 40 50 60 70 80 90 100

I am grateful for:

Day 3 | Moon Ritual | New Beginnings

A ritual to access the power of new beginnings

The light of the new moon is a portal of energy-rich with new beginnings and activations that can assist with living a life more aligned with your soul purpose and true destiny. Use the pendulum to shift subconscious blocks and jump-start some inner magic to follow your dreams that will bring more peace, joy and love.

Exercise:

Pick a number between 1 - 1000

Your number represents the number of energetic issues holding you back: resistances, hurts, negative imprints, fears, blocks, limitations, blame, shame and pain. it includes everything you can and cannot connect to relating to being held back and not moving forwards. Subconscious self-sabotage masquerades as playing it safe. The time is now to address the old issues of the past and make space for a new dawn to begin.

Using the pendulum and spin counterclockwise to access the past and say,

"I connect to and clear to zero the world of lost dreams, regrets, judgments, lost power, false limiting beliefs, struggles, the perception of lack and everything holding me back that is both conscious and subconscious from this lifetime, dimension and all past lifetimes and other dimensions."

Wait for the pendulum to stop spinning and as this is clearing energy also visualise the old clearing and dissolving away as some sort of energetic release, either as fog, smoke or colour. It will be some form of heavy energy and, however you choose to see it will be correct for you. Your body knows this is happening.

See yourself walking through a bright doorway of alchemical light

Using the pendulum clockwise to activate the new say,

"As I clear my subconscious shadows to zero, my dreams are able to evolve and I can move on as the past is now gone. I recognise myself in a brand new light about to take flight. My wisdom, drive, and flow enables me to go. I was born to progress and know that I am blessed. The releasing has energised a clearing and healing.

I take with me self-belief, self-confidence, and self-love. I know that I am guided and receiving cosmic energy from above. I now activate the wisdom and courage to try the new and all that is true. I see value in all that I am and who I can be and now that comes easily to me. I step forwards through the doorway new moon portal of light, new moon ignite my dreams so they can take flight".

Finish by thanking the moon for divine guidance and you can dowse to ask if she will be part of your spiritual team now if you both choose.

Day 3

Moon Planner

New beginnings are empowered with a ritual

Daily Intention:

What do I feel empowered to action:

Notes, ideas, commands:

What % am I ?

Focused	0 10 20 30 40 50 60 70 80 90 100
Awake	0 10 20 30 40 50 60 70 80 90 100
Aware	0 10 20 30 40 50 60 70 80 90 100
Aligned	0 10 20 30 40 50 60 70 80 90 100
Energised	0 10 20 30 40 50 60 70 80 90 100
Patient	0 10 20 30 40 50 60 70 80 90 100
Ascending	0 10 20 30 40 50 60 70 80 90 100

I am grateful for:

Day 4

Moon Ritual

Energetic Foundations

Strong energy foundations are vital for success, self-mastery & manifesting with ease.

Energetic self-care is as important as physical self-care and there are steps that can be taken each day to restore energy and vitality to healthy levels. The auric field regulates imbalances, strengthens, protects, and enables us to receive information and guidance from higher dimensions.

Empaths, healers, and lightworkers are sensitive to the energetic frequency of others and easily affected by this energy so it makes sense to be energetically free of all 'other' energy as well as clearing, repairing and strengthening the auric field.

Energy dowsing and healing

Use this checklist to check how your energy is at this time. Shock, illness, trauma, fear, lack, loss, stress can all affect our subtle energy fields and with dowsing you can test how weak or strong your energy fields are and if they need clearing, repairing or strengthening.

Dowsing to connect to your subtle energy field to locate energy checks is easy. Just ask to connect to whichever energy field you choose to, check how connected you are and then do the energy work.

As an example, if you wanted to check how grounded to mother earth you are.

Use the 0 - 100% chart and ask, "Show me how grounded I am right now."

The pendulum will move from 0 to 100% and if you are not at 100% simply ask to be 100% grounded whilst using the pendulum clockwise to activate energy. When the pendulum has stopped spinning check again and keep going until at 100%.

Energy checklist

Grounded to mother earth	0 10 20 30 40 50 60 70 80 90 100
In my body	0 10 20 30 40 50 60 70 80 90 100
Connected to higher self	0 10 20 30 40 50 60 70 80 90 100
Clear of non-beneficial energy	0 10 20 30 40 50 60 70 80 90 100
In a safe space	0 10 20 30 40 50 60 70 80 90 100
Energetically protected	0 10 20 30 40 50 60 70 80 90 100
Auric field free of nbe	0 10 20 30 40 50 60 70 80 90 100
Free of negative thoughts	0 10 20 30 40 50 60 70 80 90 100
Happy on earth	0 10 20 30 40 50 60 70 80 90 100
Free to be myself	0 10 20 30 40 50 60 70 80 90 100
Strong boundaries	0 10 20 30 40 50 60 70 80 90 100

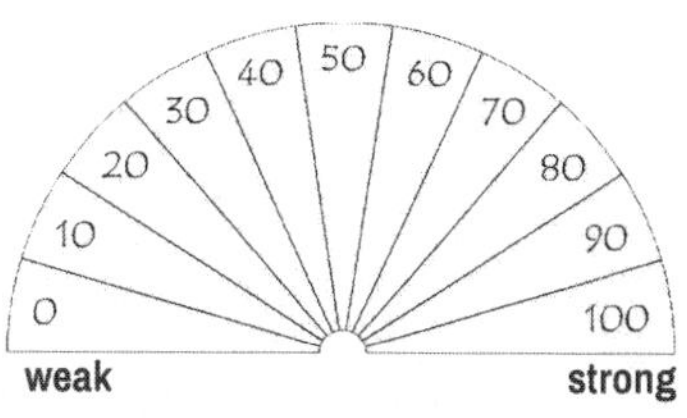

Day 4

Moon Planner

Strong energetic foundsations are the key to success

Daily Intention:

Notes on energy foundations:

Notes, ideas, commands:

What % is my/am I ?

Self-love	0 10 20 30 40 50 60 70 80 90 100
Self-care	0 10 20 30 40 50 60 70 80 90 100
Self-belief	0 10 20 30 40 50 60 70 80 90 100
Confidence	0 10 20 30 40 50 60 70 80 90 100
Self-worth	0 10 20 30 40 50 60 70 80 90 100
Speaking up	0 10 20 30 40 50 60 70 80 90 100
Happy on earth	0 10 20 30 40 50 60 70 80 90 100

I am grateful for:

Check your energetic vibrations around topics to see if you have blocks for clearing

You can check your energetic charge, flow or vibration around certain words which will show you if you have any subconscious stored blocks, fears or challenges around these topics. Dowsing lists of words can give you access to a lot of information about what may be affecting you and your ability to get things done, achieve or make plans.

For each topic ask, "Show me the energetic vibration around 'Abundance' for example.
Note it all down and we can do energy healing around any blocks relating to the words. Words carry intention and vibration and you can use them as a free form of energy for healing or clearing.

Energy topic	
Abundance	Negative - Positive
Emotional Freedom	Negative - Positive
Happiness	Negative - Positive
Empowerment	Negative - Positive
Creativity	Negative - Positive
Mindfulness	Negative - Positive
Power	Negative - Positive
Success	Negative - Positive
Freedom	Negative - Positive
Expansion	Negative - Positive
Growth	Negative - Positive
Safety	Negative - Positive
Letting go	Negative - Positive
Self-care	Negative - Positive
Self-healing	Negative - Positive
Moving forwards	Negative - Positive
Planning	Negative - Positive
Achieving	Negative - Positive
Mastery	Negative - Positive
Success	Negative - Positive

Your topics	Outcome
______________	______________
______________	______________
______________	______________
______________	______________
______________	______________
______________	______________
______________	______________
______________	______________
______________	______________
______________	______________
______________	______________
______________	______________
______________	______________
______________	______________
______________	______________
______________	______________

Command for energetic flow is below. Use the pendulum clockwise to change the energy from negative to positive.

"Restore my/the/a positive energetic flow around the area of 'abundance' for my highest good and well-being now."

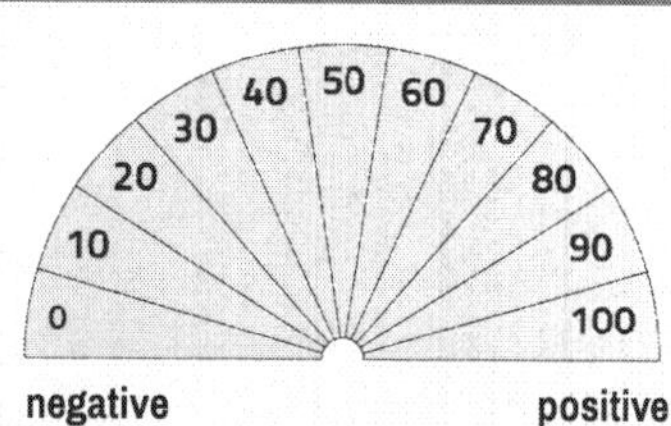

Day 5

Moon Planner

I am now in balance and feel harmony from within

Daily Intention:

Tasks:

I align with:

To Do:

Gratitude list

Check to see if energetically your giving v receiving is in balance.

Use the pendulum to check if your giving and ability to receive is open and both are in balance. Lightworkers, empaths, and healers can tend to give and give without being balanced. If we learn to accept receiving as well as giving we are living in balance and harmony.

What % is my ability to give in balance with my ability to receive?

What % can I balance this with the pendulum now for my highest good?

What % is my ability to give in balance with my ability to receive after pendulum healing?

Pendulum command counterclockwise to clear:

"I cancel all blocks, fears, and challenges stored in my energy and memory system, energetic makeup and imprinted behavior and patterns from childhood now."

Pendulum command clockwise to install:

"I now balance giving and receiving at the subconscious level of awareness. I am in balance. I know how to give as well as to receive. It is my divine right to be able to fully achieve abundance, health, wealth, love, joy and happiness in this lifetime and I now recognise this. My heart is open to all divine gifts and blessings now for my soul's growth and well-being."

Notes:

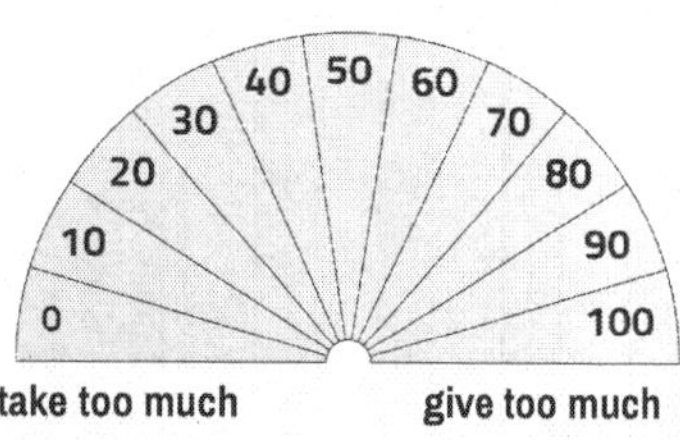

Day 7 — Moon Ritual — Practical goal setting

Use the pendulum to find out how many tasks each goal needs, whether you need to set a time frame and if you need to do it now or later. You can raise the probability of achieving the goal to 100%. Also raise confidence, self-belief, and self-love.

My goal is:

Achievable?
Worthwhile?
Long-term growth?
Short-term growth?
Does it need a timeframe?
Do I need to collaborate?
How many tasks?
Do it now or later?

My goal is:

Achievable?
Worthwhile?
Long-term growth?
Short-term growth?
Does it need a timeframe?
Do I need to collaborate?
How many tasks?
Do it now or later?

Day 7

Moon Planner

A goal without a plan is only a dream - Brian Tracy

Idea or project:

Date:	Action:	Complete:

1. Clear subconscious blocks to achieving the goal
2. Check the percentage likely to achieve the goal and increase it
3. Check if you need to collaborate or missing information
4. Check if any sabotage from self or other
5. Ask to be consciously aware of hidden variables

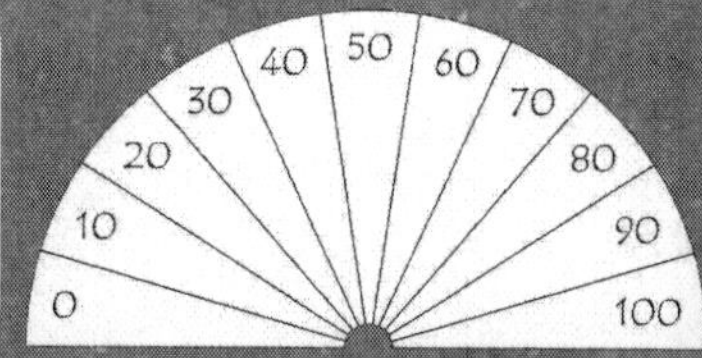

My thought intention or desire:

Some people are better at manifesting with their thoughts and others are better manifesting with the power of their emotions. You can dowse how effective your powers of manifestation are using your thoughts versus emotion and which is the most effective balance to use.

What % is this the right thought or desire for what I want to achieve?	*0 10 20 30 40 50 60 70 80 90 100*
How accurate is this for long-term happiness?	*0 10 20 30 40 50 60 70 80 90 100*
Best balance for manifesting thoughts/head?	*0 10 20 30 40 50 60 70 80 90 100*
Best balance for manifesting heart-powered?	*0 10 20 30 40 50 60 70 80 90 100*
What % can I attach a metaphysical emotion to my manifestation?	*0 10 20 30 40 50 60 70 80 90 100*

Joy	*0 10 20 30 40 50 60 70 80 90 100*
Excitement	*0 10 20 30 40 50 60 70 80 90 100*
Love	*0 10 20 30 40 50 60 70 80 90 100*
Happiness	*0 10 20 30 40 50 60 70 80 90 100*
Wonder	*0 10 20 30 40 50 60 70 80 90 100*
Trust	*0 10 20 30 40 50 60 70 80 90 100*

Which emotion is best to use?

What % do I need to clear emotional blocks to manifesting this desire?
Where from?

Resentment	*0 10 20 30 40 50 60 70 80 90 100*
Fear	*0 10 20 30 40 50 60 70 80 90 100*
Guilt	*0 10 20 30 40 50 60 70 80 90 100*
Jealousy	*0 10 20 30 40 50 60 70 80 90 100*
Despair	*0 10 20 30 40 50 60 70 80 90 100*
Helplessness	*0 10 20 30 40 50 60 70 80 90 100*
Hopelessness	*0 10 20 30 40 50 60 70 80 90 100*
Anger	*0 10 20 30 40 50 60 70 80 90 100*
Betrayal	*0 10 20 30 40 50 60 70 80 90 100*

Cells	*0 10 20 30 40 50 60 70 80 90 100*
Tissues	*0 10 20 30 40 50 60 70 80 90 100*
DNA	*0 10 20 30 40 50 60 70 80 90 100*
This timeline	*0 10 20 30 40 50 60 70 80 90 100*
Ancestral	*0 10 20 30 40 50 60 70 80 90 100*
Auric Field	*0 10 20 30 40 50 60 70 80 90 100*
Collective Conscious	*0 10 20 30 40 50 60 70 80 90 100*
Chakras	*0 10 20 30 40 50 60 70 80 90 100*

Focus on the powerful,
the euphoric & all that is ...
magical

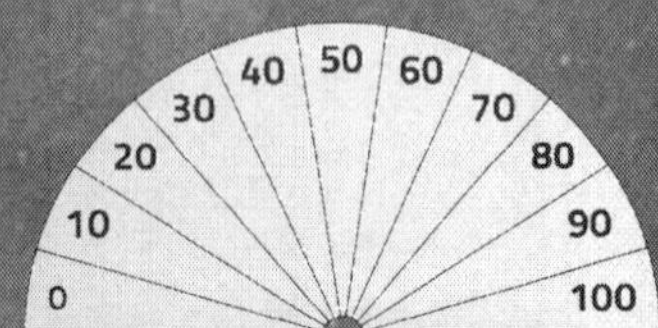

Day 8

Moon Planner

TO-DO LIST

Urgent do today	*Important do this week*
Delegate	*Discard*

How long do I need to focus on my desire for it to manifest fast?

1. Seconds
2. Minutes
3. Hours
4. Days
5. Weeks
6. Months

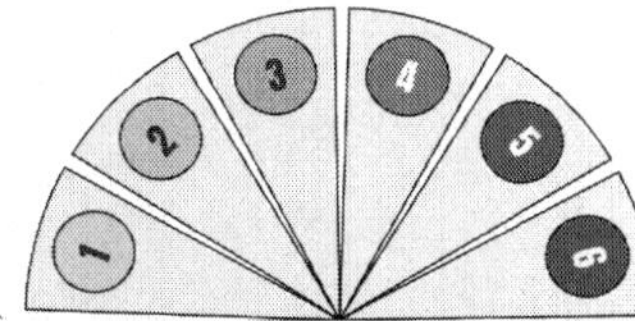

TODAY'S SCHEDULE	
6.00	
6.30	
7.00	
7.30	
8.00	
8.30	
9.00	
9.30	
10.00	
10.30	
11.00	
11.30	
12.00	
12.30	
1.00	
1.30	
2.00	
2.30	
3.00	
3.30	
4.00	
4.30	
5.00	
5.30	
6.00	
6.30	
7.00	
7.30	
8.00	
8.30	
9.00	
9.30	
10.00	
10.30	

Day 9 — Moon Ritual — Goal setting blocks

Use this chart to see if there are any obstacles in your now timeline to setting and achieving your goals, desires and dreams.

1 goals too vague
2 hard to measure
3 out of reach
4 set long-term goals
5 get goals out of head
6 do a bit each day
7 need more detailed plan
8 celebrate achievements
9 too much work involved
10 clear subc obstacles
11 magnifying fears
12 need to focus
13 lack of commitment
14 visualise achieving goals
15 need a deadline
16 need more motivation
17 look at limiting beliefs
18 self sabotage from childhood
19 procrastination
20 nothing on this chart

Goal	Blocks

Day 10 Moon Ritual Time to be Productive

How best is it energetically to spend your time?

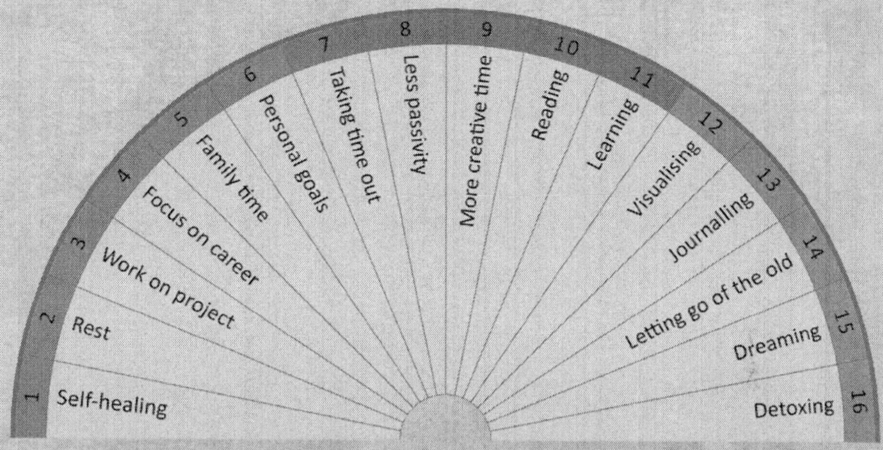

Would it be advisable to do anything on this list to be more productive? Yes/No
What % do I need to set time frames?

Self-healing	0 10 20 30 40 50 60 70 80 90 100	Be more creative	0 10 20 30 40 50 60 70 80 90 100
Rest	0 10 20 30 40 50 60 70 80 90 100	Read more	0 10 20 30 40 50 60 70 80 90 100
Work on project	0 10 20 30 40 50 60 70 80 90 100	Learn more	0 10 20 30 40 50 60 70 80 90 100
Focus on career	0 10 20 30 40 50 60 70 80 90 100	Visualise more	0 10 20 30 40 50 60 70 80 90 100
Family time	0 10 20 30 40 50 60 70 80 90 100	Journal more	0 10 20 30 40 50 60 70 80 90 100
Personal goals	0 10 20 30 40 50 60 70 80 90 100	Let go of the old	0 10 20 30 40 50 60 70 80 90 100
Take time out	0 10 20 30 40 50 60 70 80 90 100	Dreamtime	0 10 20 30 40 50 60 70 80 90 100
Be less passive	0 10 20 30 40 50 60 70 80 90 100	Time to detox	0 10 20 30 40 50 60 70 80 90 100

Day 10

Moon Planner

Short-term manifesting gaols are key for motivation

My goals:

1. ______
2. ______
3. ______
4. ______
5. ______

Daily plan	Weekly plan	Monthly plan

Day 11 | Moon Ritual | Finishing Projects

If you have a problem finishing projects you can connect to the subconscious underlying reason and clear it to zero or transmute the energy from blocked to flowing, this chart will help you pinpoint the subconscious reasons.

1. Procrastion
2. Perfectionisms
3. Fear of not being good enough
4. Childhood trauma
5. Laziness
6. Disorganised
7. No deadlines
8. Putting tasks off
9. Low self-belief
10. Resistance
11. Too many projects
12. Too scattered
13. No Goals
14. Fear of tomorrow
15. Giving up too easily

Use the same chart to find out what could be a possible solution to resolving the above problems around not finishing projects.

"Regarding the project/goal/task of ________ show me what will be most useful for me to finish the task."

1. Clear fear of today, yesterday & tomorrow
2. Clear negative projections from others
3. Remove fears and judgments from self/others
4. Cancel inner saboteur/inner critic
5. Organise time better
6. Focus on one thing at a time
7. Just need to start
8. Vision the end goal & ask source for help
9. Create an astral vision board
10. Remove inner resistance
11. Clear belief that it is too hard
12. Clear belief that it's not possible
13. Clear belief that you are unworthy
14. Look at burnout and do less
15. Use pendulum to organise tasks into priority

Day 11

Moon Planner

Track your short-term and long-term goals for success

short-term

	Goal	Action step
Personal		
Professional		
Financial		
Other		

Personal		
Professional		
Financial		
Other		

long-term

Day 12 **Moon Ritual** **Working Smarter**

Working smarter instead of harder

Use this chart to see if there are any areas where you need to work smarter and not harder, rate them as a percentage so you can keep track of the most sabotaging behaviors!

Would it be adviseable to do anything on this list to be more productive? Yes/No
What % do I need to set time frames?

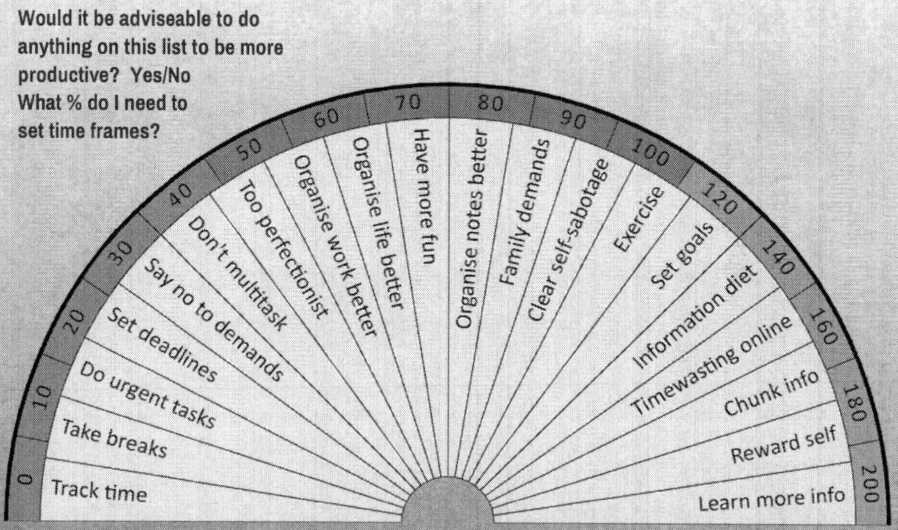

Organise notes better	0 10 20 30 40 50 60 70 80 90 100	Track my time
Say no to family	0 10 20 30 40 50 60 70 80 90 100	Take more breaks
Clear self-sabotage	0 10 20 30 40 50 60 70 80 90 100	Do urgent tasks
Exercise	0 10 20 30 40 50 60 70 80 90 100	Set deadlines
Set more goals	0 10 20 30 40 50 60 70 80 90 100	Say no to demands
Information diet	0 10 20 30 40 50 60 70 80 90 100	Don't multi-task
Less time surfing	0 10 20 30 40 50 60 70 80 90 100	Be less perfectionist
Chunk information	0 10 20 30 40 50 60 70 80 90 100	Organise work better
Reward self	0 10 20 30 40 50 60 70 80 90 100	Organise life better
Learn more	0 10 20 30 40 50 60 70 80 90 100	Have more fun

Day 12

Moon Planner

Plan your projects for success

Project planner

Action steps:

Due Date:

Progress:

Day 13

Moon Ritual

Planetary Energy

Using the consciousness of planetary vibrations for power, energy & focus

Dowse the energetic frequency of the planet that can help you achieve success in one or many areas of your life. We contain the elements of the planets within us. It is easy to connect to the energetic frequency of a planetary source of energy by simply asking to do so.

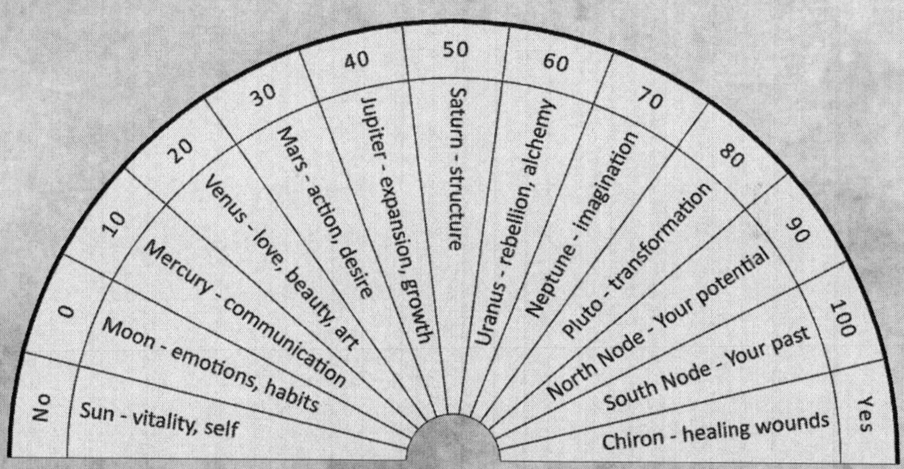

1. Dowse the planetary energy best suited to help with a challenge
2. Ask to connect to the energetic frequency
3. Check the % connected
4. Receive messages or run a pendulum command
5. Check the % the energy will have helped you, disconnect & thank the planet

The issue I want to resolve is:

The planet I most need to work with is:

The planet that wants to work with me is:

The signs of the zodiac are karmic patterns; the planets are the looms; the will is the weaver. ~Author Unknown

Day 13

Moon Planner

Planetary & task tracker

I need to focus on:

Finances	0 10 20 30 40 50 60 70 80 90 100
Self-care	0 10 20 30 40 50 60 70 80 90 100
Confidence	0 10 20 30 40 50 60 70 80 90 100
Social life	0 10 20 30 40 50 60 70 80 90 100
Career/Business	0 10 20 30 40 50 60 70 80 90 100
Study	0 10 20 30 40 50 60 70 80 90 100
My environment	0 10 20 30 40 50 60 70 80 90 100
Alchemy	0 10 20 30 40 50 60 70 80 90 100
Comfort zone	0 10 20 30 40 50 60 70 80 90 100
Inner Child healing	0 10 20 30 40 50 60 70 80 90 100
Diet/Exercise	0 10 20 30 40 50 60 70 80 90 100
Grounding	0 10 20 30 40 50 60 70 80 90 100

Planetary energy notes

Using planetary energy:

Connect within
Look at a photo
Use the planetary hours
Water imprint with pic
Clear old energy
Use planet sigils for healing
Ask for divine guidance
Learn about planets

What % is this challenging me to grow?

Day 14 Moon Ritual The Goddess

Use this chart to see which Goddess wants to work with you today, are you fully honouring all aspects of your inner goddess, your beauty, your wisdom, and power? Connecting to and invoking the goddess energy can help you to connect to these inner aspects within us for power, strength and healing.

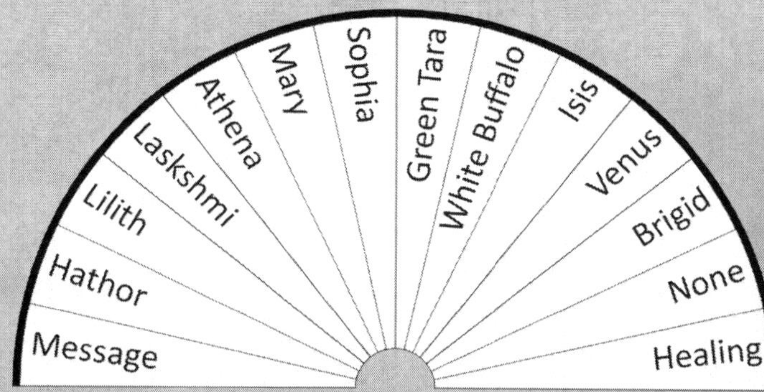

Dowse to see which Goddess wants to give you a message and which wants to give you an energetic healing.

1. Hathor	Access your inner light, finding beauty
2. Lilith	Helps discover power in the darkness
3. Lakshmi	Wealth activation and gifts
4. Athena	wisdom, communication & protection
5. Mary	Inner healing power
6. Sophia	Intuition & creativity
7. Green Tara	Protection & safety
8. White Buffalo	Finding the correct soul mate
9. Isis	Healing, Magic, and Wisdom
10. Venus	Discovering beauty & strength
11. Brigid	Fertility, crafts, creativity and new beginnings

- Ask the Goddesses to see your inner beauty
- Ask them to bless the water you drink
- Connect to Venus for anti-aging commands
- Ask for blessings and gifts to be activated in your now timeline
- Do a ritual and send them love from your heart space
- Create a loving mantra in their honour and bless your house
- Ask to uncover lost or hidden knowledge, energy and power
- Create a healing circle, invite them all and send love to Mother Earth
- Increase trust in yourself and your ability to change the world
- Ask them to guide you and bring you deep soul connections based on love

I am my own sacred light – I honour the goddess within

Day 14

Moon Planner

Messages from the goddess within

Speak through the heart of your inner goddess:

Honour the wisdom that lies within

Day 15 Moon Ritual The Archangels

Use this chart to see which Archangel wants to work with you today or ask to connect to the energetic frequency of one. Check using the pendulum that you are connected with their energy and activate the right conditions for inspiration, downloads and messages or support.

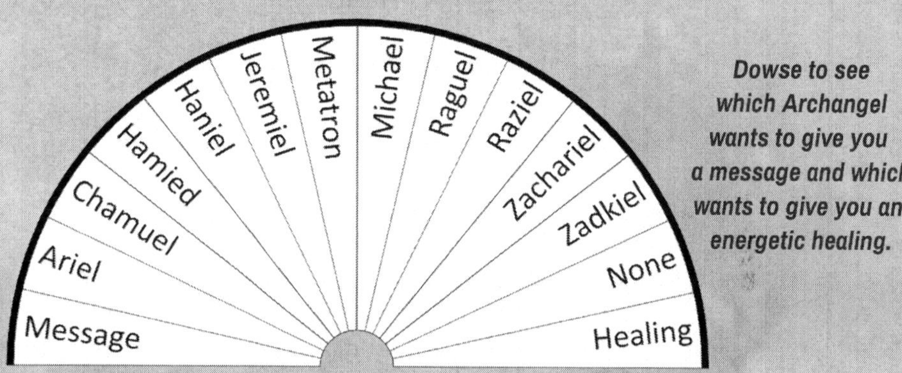

Dowse to see which Archangel wants to give you a message and which wants to give you an energetic healing.

1. Ariel	Helps start a business or finding a job
2. Chamuel	Increases self-esteem, belief, self-awareness
3. Hamied	Aligns with miracles and magic
4. Haniel	Clears past wounds and emotional upsets
5. Jeremiel	Problem solver and inspires taking action
6. Metatron	Helps to find inner gifts and passions
7. Michael	Protection, courage, and inspiration
8. Raguel	Healing money worries
9. Raziel	Divine magic, manifesting prosperity
10. Zachariel	Clears self-sabotage and inner blocks
11. Zadkiel	Activates inner life purpose and path

Ask the Archangels to clear doubt, lack, shame and blame around money
Ask them to raise your vibration in alignment with your inner desires
Ask them to send you blessings easily seen on your life path
Ask them to bring you clients, people, and new opportunities
Let them know you are thankful and send them blessings
Ask that you see yourself as you truely are, a wonder of divine light and love
Ask to clear cycles of poverty, scarcity, fear, and resistance to money
Ask them to help clear debts, doubts, worries and activate hidden resource streams of wealth
Ask the % you are manifesting lack and to reverse that
Ask the % you are responsible for your own health, wealth & happiness and if not at 100% raise it

Allow yourself to remember and be guided with light

Day 16

Moon Ritual

Commanding Achievements

Use the pendulum to check if anything is blocking your ability to achieve and the percentage. It is possible to connect to the block metaphysically without needing to know what they are. Your subconscious awareness will know and you will be connected simply by asking to connect.

Exercise

This exercise will enable you to connect to the root cause of your inability to achieve or the root cause of your inability to celebrate your achievements.

1. Ask to be connected to the root cause of your inability to achieve or notice your achievements.
2. Check if you are connected to the root cause and receive a YES.
3. If you receive a NO use the pendulum to spin counterclockwise and ask to clear all obstacles.
4. When fully connected to the root cause spin the pendulum counterclockwise and use this command:

"I dissolve all past energy blocks holding me back. All negative influences from the past are now null and void. Childhood blocks and negative conditioning causing limitations are gone, dissolved and now resolved. In the area of ______ I am now free".

5. Wait for the pendulum to stop spinning and check the % you have just cleared the blocks.
6. If not at 100% clear, keep spinning counterclockwise and ask to connect to every limitation.
7. Replace the void with some positive energetic power using this command and spinning the pendulum clockwise:

"I now transform the energy of I can't to I can and will, I receive the ability to achieve my heart's desire in the area of _______. I am free to believe that I can achieve with ease."

NO YES

Pendulum Commands

I am on the path of success, I am transformed, healthy and whole
I am innovative, inventive and creative, I know how to achieve my personal power
I am willing, ready, and able to action my dreams now
I see what was hidden, I am aware of the next step,
I am in harmony and co-create with ease and grace, I know how to prioritise
My negotiating skills are raised to the highest level,
I take full responsibility for my life now
I am imaginative, creative and resourceful, I am pure energy
I have emotional balance and freedom to achieve and then receive
I now easily access my inner gifts and talents that make me unique
I know that I create my own reality and heart's desire.

Day 16

Moon Planner

Celebrate your achievements, what has gone well this week

What will go brilliantly next week?

Look in the mirror and tell yourself how amazing you are at least once a day

What % are you happy with your achievements?
Do you celebrate your achievements?
What % would it be good to keep an achievements journal?
What % are you proud of yourself?

Day 17 Moon Ritual Self-esteem

With confidence in your own worth and value, you can achieve anything you desire, this begins with having high self-esteem.

Questions

Question	Scale
What % was my self-esteem damaged at childhood?	0 10 20 30 40 50 60 70 80 90 100
What % do I believe in my inner value and worth?	0 10 20 30 40 50 60 70 80 90 100
What % do I listen to others over myself?	0 10 20 30 40 50 60 70 80 90 100
What % am I able to assert myself?	0 10 20 30 40 50 60 70 80 90 100
What % do I avoid difficult situations or people?	0 10 20 30 40 50 60 70 80 90 100
What % do I treat myself badly?	0 10 20 30 40 50 60 70 80 90 100
What % do I stand up for my beliefs?	0 10 20 30 40 50 60 70 80 90 100
What % do I show myself, love?	0 10 20 30 40 50 60 70 80 90 100

Pendulum commands:

Transform the idea of having to be liked by others into loving myself absolutely
Enable me to believe in myself and my truth absolutely
Raise my ability to connect with others easily and be ok
Enable me to expect more out of life and go get it
I now receive missing love, respect, trust, self-belief, and confidence missing from childhood
I transform all worry and concern around what people think of me
I respect my own judgment and truth and know that I am amazing
I clear all worries around getting things wrong
I love life and know how to experiment with energy
I know that I am safe and loved

Exercise:

Connect to your heart space and use the pendulum to check how aligned you are with these statements. If you are less than 100% use the statements as a pendulum command and raise to 100%

I expect to achieve my dreams
I trust my opinions
I am valuable
I am proud of my achievements
I can handle criticism
I know my positive qualities
I focus on my success

I believe in myself
I have a supportive network
I appreciate who I am
It's easy for me to try new things
I assert my boundaries
I easily take risks
I am confident in new situations

"Connect to the root cause of energetically not seeing my own self-worth and transform."

Day 17

Moon Planner

Write down some amazing things that you have done, you are currently doing and that you will do.

Amazing things I've done

Amazing things I'm doing

Amazing things I will do

Day 18 **Moon Ritual** **self-belief**

Self-criticising is tied to low self-esteem, perfectionism and a lack of self-belief.
Dowse to see how you feel about yourself so you can break
out of old habits and thought patterns holding you back.

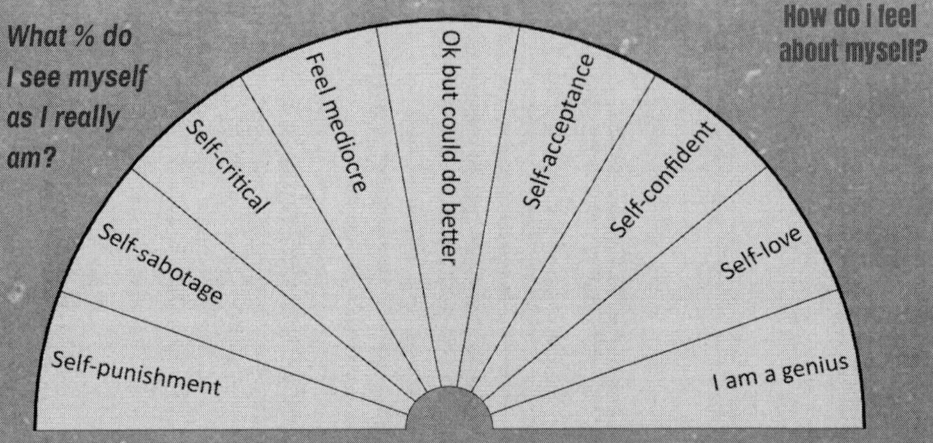

What % of the time do you engage in these behaviours?

Not having boundaries that support you	0 10 20 30 40 50 60 70 80 90 100
Negative self-talk	0 10 20 30 40 50 60 70 80 90 100
Don't stand up for yourself	0 10 20 30 40 50 60 70 80 90 100
Being indecisive	0 10 20 30 40 50 60 70 80 90 100
Frustration with time	0 10 20 30 40 50 60 70 80 90 100
Overly detailed	0 10 20 30 40 50 60 70 80 90 100
Comparing self to others	0 10 20 30 40 50 60 70 80 90 100
Not aligned with higher self	0 10 20 30 40 50 60 70 80 90 100
Fear limitations	0 10 20 30 40 50 60 70 80 90 100
Thinking of the past	0 10 20 30 40 50 60 70 80 90 100
Childhood trauma	0 10 20 30 40 50 60 70 80 90 100
Angry at choosing this life	0 10 20 30 40 50 60 70 80 90 100
Don't support self energetically	0 10 20 30 40 50 60 70 80 90 100
Not protecting daily from nbe	0 10 20 30 40 50 60 70 80 90 100
Too much to do at once	0 10 20 30 40 50 60 70 80 90 100
Not clearing old things out	0 10 20 30 40 50 60 70 80 90 100
Not having support networks	0 10 20 30 40 50 60 70 80 90 100

Mirror healing can help with self-trust, self-love, & taking back inner power

The energetic frequency of buttercup enables you to break out of old patterns and allows your gifts & talents to shine

Day 18

Moon Planner

Write out your negative self-beliefs so you can clear them from your energy field, timeline and lifetime.

On a separate piece of paper that you can burn or throw away write out all the negative beliefs about yourself that you can think of.

Using a pendulum counterclockwise ask to remove the beliefs from your energy and memory system with this command or one similar:

"Remove these negative self-beliefs from my energy and memory system, all negative self-beliefs not serving my highest good are transformed into their equal and highest opposite now".

See the energy of the beliefs and words flying out of your energy system as you use the pendulum and say the command. They are leaving your energy system for good.

Self-care
Confidence
Wisdom
Self-love
Self-worth
Visibility
Inner peace
Vibrancy
Happiness
Self-esteem

See a golden ball of shimmering energetic light which shifts and disconnects you from all negative energy, frozen emotions, and negative cycles and time loops keeping you stuck.

See these positive words fly into your energy system as you spin the pendulum clockwise, see them as activational and motivational energies coming into powerfully assist you.

" I replace all fear with love in my holographic energy field. Ideas, information and insight are freely available to me as i ground and anchor my light energy now."

You are a receiver of universal light energy & power.
You are grounded, balanced, centered, anchored and whole.
See a golden anchor placed from your feet into the earth. You are safe and able to accept any earth healing that you need to receive from Mother Earth now.

Day 19 Moon Ritual Inner Power

Clearing blocks to standing in your power

Inner power relates to the Solar Plexus chakra so we can ask how much is the solar plexus clear and free of other people's energy, beliefs, ideas, demands and control structures. It will be more beneficial to be 100% free energetically of this.

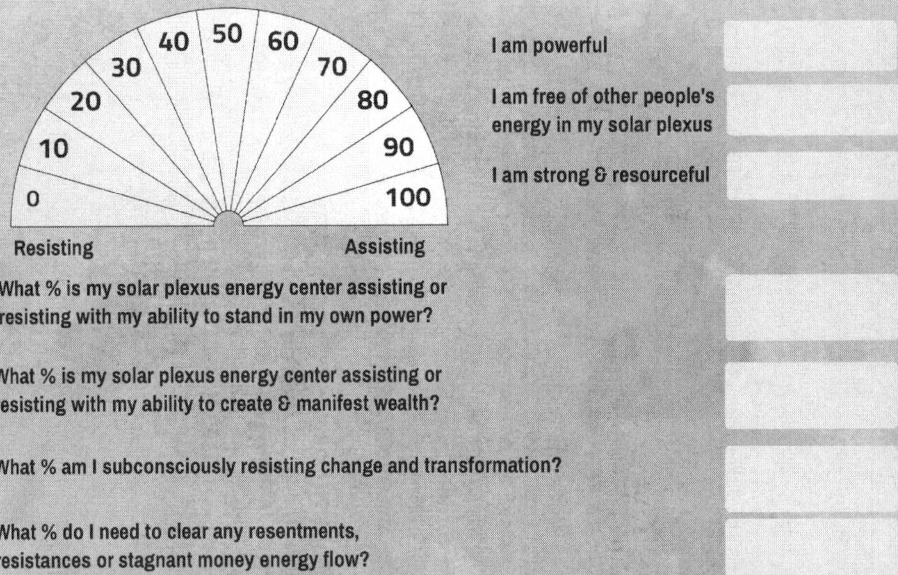

I am powerful

I am free of other people's energy in my solar plexus

I am strong & resourceful

What % is my solar plexus energy center assisting or resisting with my ability to stand in my own power?

What % is my solar plexus energy center assisting or resisting with my ability to create & manifest wealth?

What % am I subconsciously resisting change and transformation?

What % do I need to clear any resentments, resistances or stagnant money energy flow?

"I now clear blocked, limiting and powerless energy from myself and others residing in my solar plexus blocking me and stopping me from achieving my goals, dreams, and desires."

"Activate and strengthen solar plexus energy with new power, confidence, self-belief and manifesting mastery ability, I know subconsciously I can achieve my goals and dreams and this is imprinted in the Akashic, shadow, inner child and, subconscious levels of my reality now."

Receive a message from your solar plexus?

Day 19

Moon Planner

Reflections on the journey so far:

What has gone well? Any positive unexpected developments?

Day 20 | Moon Ritual | Energetic Flow

Use this chart to see if anything is blocking, trapping or stopping the energetic flow around your energy or the energy of your business. Find out if your energy, focus, and power is limited or expansive.

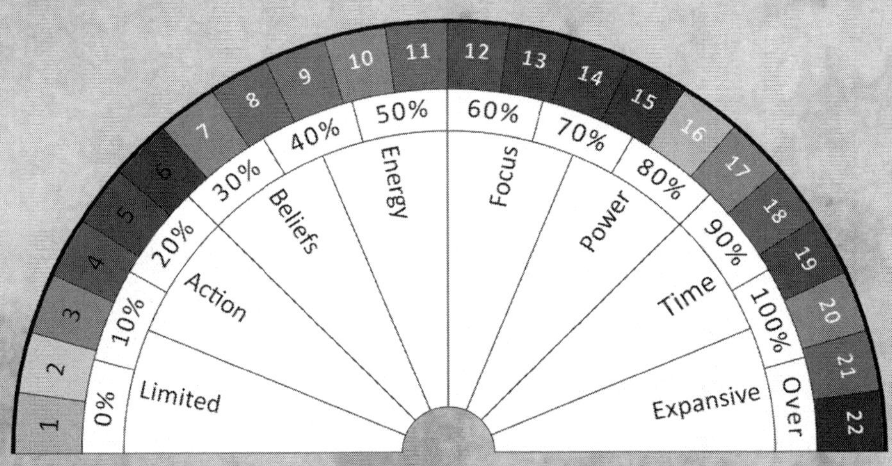

1. Subconscious fears
2. Procrastination
3. Other people
4. Low confidence
5. Imprints/Implants
6. Visibility issues
7. Curses/Cords/Tags
8. Stress/Burnout
9. Low motivation
10. Ancestral imprints
11. Auric field needs repair
12. Not grounded
13. Not in the body
14. Planetary energy
15. Self sabotage
16. Low self-belief
17. Feel like a failure
18. Creative insecurity
19. Inherited negative emotions
20. Childhood conditioning
21. Doing too much at once
22. Nothing impeding flow

To increase my manifesting power what do I need to be focusing on?

To correct any negative energy flow simply ask to disconnect from the energy or trigger causing the issue and use the pendulum counterclockwise to clear it.

Check the percentages before and after the healing to see that your energy healing has worked.

Day 20

Moon Planner

Actions to take:

Beliefs to clear:

My energy is:

My time and focus needs to be:

Day 21 Moon Ritual Core Blocks

Is anything is energetically blocking you or stopping you from achieving abundance or financial success in this now lifetime and timeline.

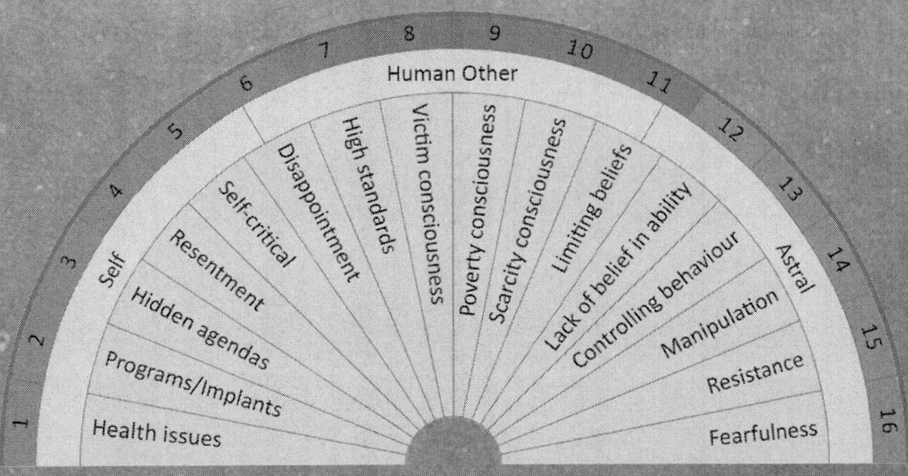

Pendulum command counterclockwise to clear:

"Connect to all and everything on this chart causing financial and monetary limitations and sabotage relating to my ability to make money and be financially prosperous in this lifetime and timeline. I am now free of these influences and able to live my life standing in my power."

Clockwise to activate the new:

"It is my divine right to be happy, healthy and financially free in this timeline and lifetime. My timeline is reset to achieving financial prosperity and independence in this lifetime with ease and wonder, new ways of making money easily come to me now, this is my divine right."

Day 21

Moon Planner

Reflections on the journey so far:

Day 22 — Moon Ritual — Going deeper

Going deeper into the process of manifesting means having clarity at every stage of the journey to see exactly where you are and what may need to be done.

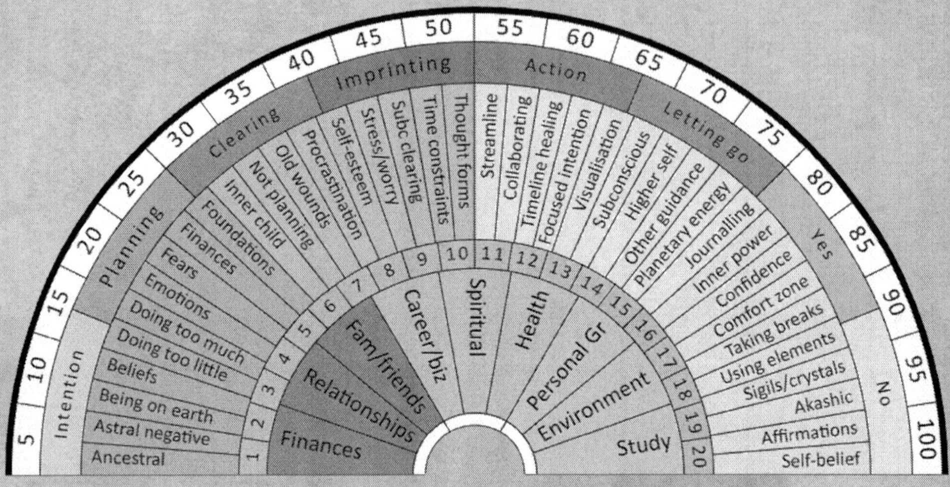

Questions to ask:

What stage of the manifesting process am I at?

Is there anything blocking my progress? YES/NO What is it?

How positive is my current timeine for manifesting?

Positive next step to take?

What % am I blocked at the level of belief?

How do I receive wisdom?

How many days at each stage is best?

Intention		Imprinting	
Planning		Action	
Clearing		Letting go	

Day 22

Moon Planner

Notes from the dowsing session:

Day 23 Moon Ritual Sub-conscious Beliefs

It is easy to connect to and reprogram subconscious beliefs with the pendulum and one of the most powerful ways to access new information and heightened awareness. No need now to listen to hours of repetitive music or go into a trance to achieve fast transformations.

The subconscious stores all the information that ever existed, all our habits, blocks and fears. Connecting to and clearing the negatives from this stored data will not only enable us to move on from challenges but stop the repetitive cyclic habitual programs that plague us and keep us trapped in the past.

Dowse to see if you can change your subconscious beliefs using a pendulum? Yes No

Pendulum command counterclockwise to clear subconscious beliefs:

"Connect to and disconnect from ALL subconscious beliefs, worries and limiting thoughts not supporting me around the area of MONEY. All past traps, vows, cords, tags, beliefs, subconscious conditioning are now NULL and VOID."

The pendulum will spin counterclockwise to clear non-beneficial beliefs.
Wait for it to stop spinning before testing using a 0 - 100% chart to find out what % the beliefs are affecting you now.

Clockwise to activate the new:

"My subconscious is now back on track and aligned with my conscious desires around the area of MONEY. I see swift and fast progress in this and all areas of life relating to this command."

Areas to look at:

Money	0 10 20 30 40 50 60 70 80 90 100
Freedom	0 10 20 30 40 50 60 70 80 90 100
Self-love	0 10 20 30 40 50 60 70 80 90 100
Confidence	0 10 20 30 40 50 60 70 80 90 100
Self-worth	0 10 20 30 40 50 60 70 80 90 100
Self-healing	0 10 20 30 40 50 60 70 80 90 100
Taking risks	0 10 20 30 40 50 60 70 80 90 100
Comfort zone	0 10 20 30 40 50 60 70 80 90 100
Ability to receive	0 10 20 30 40 50 60 70 80 90 100

In the area of ______ are my subconscious beliefs empowering or inhibiting?

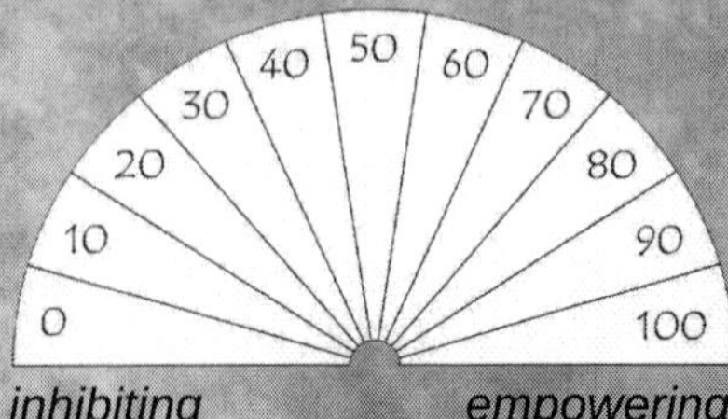

Day 23

Moon Planner

YOUR BELIEFS ARE MATTER

A pendulum is a tool for self-development and empowerment using light.

- We are all made of light
- I believe in the creative force of nature
- We are all connected at a higher level
- We can change timelines and lifetimes
- Our body responds to our thoughts
- The universe hears our thoughts
- We can leave ourselves gifts of love
- Each day is a new beginning of play
- Clearing blocks, challenges and fears is fun
- We can turn genes on or off
- We can change the past to heal the present
- Energy is accessed through picture, words and intention

I believe that:

Day 24 Moon Ritual self-beliefs

Any self-beliefs not congruent with your goals and dreams will be limiting you in some way. You can test lists and sets of beliefs to see if they are affecting your ability to manifest, have the life you want or increase wealth for example.

You can shift the energy around the negative self-beliefs with a pendulum command and spinning the pendulum counterclockwise:

"Clear all my unhelpful and limiting self-beliefs and subconscious self-sabotage around the statement, "Money is easy to make" or "I stand in my own power."

You can do a mass clearing of everything on this worksheet if you choose to or clear the limiting beliefs one by one. I choose to do them at once - fast but it is your decision with what you feel comfortable doing.

list of negative self-beliefs

I'm not good enough	0 10 20 30 40 50 60 70 80 90 100
I don't get support	0 10 20 30 40 50 60 70 80 90 100
My childhood was lacking	0 10 20 30 40 50 60 70 80 90 100
My foundations are not solid	0 10 20 30 40 50 60 70 80 90 100
I can't rely on others	0 10 20 30 40 50 60 70 80 90 100
I'm blocked from making money	0 10 20 30 40 50 60 70 80 90 100
I am unlovable	0 10 20 30 40 50 60 70 80 90 100
I don't deserve success	0 10 20 30 40 50 60 70 80 90 100
I can't be myself	0 10 20 30 40 50 60 70 80 90 100
I don't have enough time	0 10 20 30 40 50 60 70 80 90 100
I'm not worthy of love	0 10 20 30 40 50 60 70 80 90 100
I can't express who I am	0 10 20 30 40 50 60 70 80 90 100
I'll never amount to anything	0 10 20 30 40 50 60 70 80 90 100
Life is such a struggle	0 10 20 30 40 50 60 70 80 90 100
I hate change	0 10 20 30 40 50 60 70 80 90 100
I'm anxious about the future	0 10 20 30 40 50 60 70 80 90 100
I'll never be successful	0 10 20 30 40 50 60 70 80 90 100
No one listens to me	0 10 20 30 40 50 60 70 80 90 100
I can't make my own choices	0 10 20 30 40 50 60 70 80 90 100

"As I clear my negative self-beliefs from point of conception I am now more positively aligned with my soul gifts, inner power and ability to speak my truth."

Another clearing command could be, "Scramble every limiting false belief from myself and others affecting my timeline and lifetime now."

If at a subconscious level you believe yourself to be intelligent, capable, wise and a genius of the highest order then could your brainwaves activate the ability to receive more information from higher frequency thought?

Day 24

Moon Planner

Write some positive beliefs and imprint them into your subconscious awareness, " I imprint my subconscious awareness, reality and behaviour with the belief that _____."

I am:

Day 25

Moon Ritual

Money beliefs

As well as self-beliefs, beliefs around the world it is also possible to check your beliefs around money and clear any unhelpful, harmful or subconsciously negative beliefs and fears around money blocking you from making money or manifesting.

list of negative money beliefs:

Money is evil/bad	0 10 20 30 40 50 60 70 80 90 100
Money corrupts people	0 10 20 30 40 50 60 70 80 90 100
Money is difficult to make and keep	0 10 20 30 40 50 60 70 80 90 100
There not enough to go round	0 10 20 30 40 50 60 70 80 90 100
I can't be spiritual and rich	0 10 20 30 40 50 60 70 80 90 100
Life is a slog	0 10 20 30 40 50 60 70 80 90 100
I'll always be broke, it's too hard	0 10 20 30 40 50 60 70 80 90 100
Financial security is only a dream	0 10 20 30 40 50 60 70 80 90 100
I can't afford that	0 10 20 30 40 50 60 70 80 90 100
I'm always in debt	0 10 20 30 40 50 60 70 80 90 100
I'm not good at handling money	0 10 20 30 40 50 60 70 80 90 100
Rich people aren't happy	0 10 20 30 40 50 60 70 80 90 100
You have to work hard to have money	0 10 20 30 40 50 60 70 80 90 100
I can't ever get onto things	0 10 20 30 40 50 60 70 80 90 100
The cost of living is so high	0 10 20 30 40 50 60 70 80 90 100
It's hard to hold onto money	0 10 20 30 40 50 60 70 80 90 100
There's a limit to how much I can earn	0 10 20 30 40 50 60 70 80 90 100
I'm afraid to ask for what I want	0 10 20 30 40 50 60 70 80 90 100
Life is a struggle	0 10 20 30 40 50 60 70 80 90 100
I'm blocking my ability to manifest	0 10 20 30 40 50 60 70 80 90 100

"I ground, anchor & center my abiity to create money. I now clear all programs of lack, scarcity and poverty. I clear all anxiety, frustration and insecurity around having and not having now."

Money is simply energy but it is your attitude and subconscious beliefs that make it easy or hard for you to attract.

You can also ask to disconnect from any negative triggers in your timeline around money or clear negative subconscious patterns keeping you trapped in disappointment and fear.

Dowse how ready you are on a scale of 0 - 100% to shift your relationship with money.

Connect your ability to earn money with freedom, ease, grace, harmony and love. Activate positive triggers or align positively with the energy of money in your timeline in this lifetime.

Imprint this command into your now reality, "I am ready, I am aware, I am focused on inner and outer wealth creation with ease and grace, I make physical form from thought."

Day 25

Moon Planner

Write your own positive money story:

I connect to magical success
My powers of manifestation have increased 10 fold
I connect my intelligence, wisdom and ground my new found ideas
I see a magical intelligence at work in my bank account
My happiness contains the energy and elements of abundance, magic & freedom

Day 26

Moon Ritual

Fears blocking manifesting

Clearing your deepest fears and negative programming at the subconscious level will hugely increase your ability to manifest. When you clear doubts, blocks and fears you free yourself to be the infinite creator you have
always been.

Fears for clearing:

Fear of financial power	0 10 20 30 40 50 60 70 80 90 100	
Fear of having money	0 10 20 30 40 50 60 70 80 90 100	
Fear of not having money	0 10 20 30 40 50 60 70 80 90 100	
Fear that money is hard to come by	0 10 20 30 40 50 60 70 80 90 100	What % is this fear affecting my ability to be financially wealthy in this now lifetime?
Negative money programming	0 10 20 30 40 50 60 70 80 90 100	
Money is a sacred resource	0 10 20 30 40 50 60 70 80 90 100	
Regressive projections	0 10 20 30 40 50 60 70 80 90 100	
Regressive perceptions	0 10 20 30 40 50 60 70 80 90 100	
Reward only after effort	0 10 20 30 40 50 60 70 80 90 100	
Famine consciousness	0 10 20 30 40 50 60 70 80 90 100	
Poverty consciousness	0 10 20 30 40 50 60 70 80 90 100	
Prisoner consciousness	0 10 20 30 40 50 60 70 80 90 100	

Fears & Beliefs for clearing:

Poor but honest	0 10 20 30 40 50 60 70 80 90 100	
Not having enough	0 10 20 30 40 50 60 70 80 90 100	
Not being good enough	0 10 20 30 40 50 60 70 80 90 100	
Childhood conditioning	0 10 20 30 40 50 60 70 80 90 100	
Limiting beliefs from parents	0 10 20 30 40 50 60 70 80 90 100	
Ancestral lack woven into money story	0 10 20 30 40 50 60 70 80 90 100	What % are you repelling wealth?
Social control	0 10 20 30 40 50 60 70 80 90 100	
Can't be rich and spiritual	0 10 20 30 40 50 60 70 80 90 100	
Gifts are supposed to be free	0 10 20 30 40 50 60 70 80 90 100	
Can't trust self or others	0 10 20 30 40 50 60 70 80 90 100	
Fear of yesterday, today and tomorrow	0 10 20 30 40 50 60 70 80 90 100	Aligned with wealth?
Push/pull wealth cycle	0 10 20 30 40 50 60 70 80 90 100	
Money will trap me	0 10 20 30 40 50 60 70 80 90 100	
Worry about having money	0 10 20 30 40 50 60 70 80 90 100	
Money will change me	0 10 20 30 40 50 60 70 80 90 100	
I will lose my friends	0 10 20 30 40 50 60 70 80 90 100	

"I now erase old programs, paradigms and conditioning templates
not serving my highest good around being successful.
I release struggle and cellular lack programs.
My subconscious now vibrates and aligns with fast success."

Day 26

Moon Planner

Clearing fears tracker

My fears, blocks & challenges	% clear

Day 27 **Moon Ritual** **Business Goals**

Clearing blocks and making decisions around your business goals is easy and fun using the pendulum. You can literally fast-track yourself to success.

My business goal/idea is:

What % am I on track with this idea/goal?	0 10 20 30 40 50 60 70 80 90 100
What % do I need to outsource?	0 10 20 30 40 50 60 70 80 90 100
What % do I need to collaborate?	0 10 20 30 40 50 60 70 80 90 100
What % am I able to start and succeed in my own business?	0 10 20 30 40 50 60 70 80 90 100
What % am I offering what my clients will want?	0 10 20 30 40 50 60 70 80 90 100
What % is this the right idea for me now?	0 10 20 30 40 50 60 70 80 90 100
How realistically can I achieve my dream business in this lifetime?	0 10 20 30 40 50 60 70 80 90 100

Pendulum commands for self-empowerment around business:

I easily tap into new skills that I need to create the business I desire
I am proud of my ideas and achievements in business
I receive creative ideas that sell and come to me easily
I meet others who share my vision, we help each other
I set achievable goals and effortlessly complete them
I experience new business powers to achieve success
Enable me to easily learn from challenges
Creative new opportunities appear at my door as if by magic
My business moves forth in fun and interesting ways
I experience an explosion of confidence and creativity with happiness and joy
I am filled with peace, love, hope and calm, this is so easy for me
I allow my innate skills, talents and gifts to shine and be easily accessible
My energy flows and knows what I need to do, every cell in my body supports new growth
Manifesting and marketing easily fall into place and I transform I can't to I can and I am
I have the energy, insight, clarity and resources to easily attract opportunities into my timeline
Clients easily find me and can afford me, I know I am helped with getting a business off the ground

Day 27

Moon Planner

Business planner

Strategy List

Meetings to organise

Calls to make

Collaborate
Outsource
Keep planning
Clear resistance
Manage your time

Day 28 - Time to reflect

Congratulations you have completed your 28-day moon manifesting journey. It is now time to reflect and look inwards. Some of your manifestations will have come in and some will be ready to come in the next moon cycle or the cycles afterwards.

Expansion is where the growth and magic lies so build upon your successes and achievements this cycle to create more personal challenges that lead you outside your comfort zone.

What are you most proud of?

What went well over the last 28 days?

What will you do differently next moon cycle?

Next steps & challenges

Don't limit your challenges, challenge your limits

Having a fulfilled life means to be regularly challenged and leaving your comfort zone creates a wealth of inner strength, magic and opportunity. The author cycled around South America for 6 months when she was 24 having never been on a bike before she arrived in Caracas.

Believe in the power of your dreams, go forwards and fly.

Over the next 6 months I will be:

Challenge 1:

Challenge 2:

Challenge 3:

Challenge 4:

Challenge 5:

Challenge 6:

Full Moon Dates - 2019

21st Jan - Resourcefulness
19th Feb - Purification
21st Mar - Affirming bonds
19th Apr - Growth & magic
18th May - Fertility
17th Jun - Bliss filled love
16th July - Planning
15th Aug - Honour ancestors
14th Sep - Mother Earth
13th Oct - Mystery & power
12th Nov - Death of the old
12th Dec - Endings

If you would like to learn more about pendulum dowsing and how to use the pendulum as a healing tool:

https://thedivinationpath.thinkific.com/courses/the-pendulum-healing-course

If you would like to find out about the launch of new books and divination decks:

https://www.facebook.com/groups/theartofmanifesting/

Happy dowsing and manifesting with the moon.

Melissa Tessaro

Made in the USA
Columbia, SC
20 December 2022

74661497R00054